①3967
Aust.

2 00

CW00530448

Seafaring 1939–45
as I saw it

Seafaring 1939–45 as I saw it

Captain R. F. McBrearty MN

The Pentland Press
Edinburgh – Cambridge – Durham

To my wife, Miriam

© R. F. McBrearty, 1995

First published in 1995 by
The Pentland Press Ltd
1 Hutton Close
South Church
Bishop Auckland
Durham

All rights reserved.
Unauthorised duplication
contravenes existing laws

ISBN 1-85821-282-0

Typeset by Carnegie Publishing, 18 Maynard St., Preston
Printed and bound by Antony Rowe Ltd., Chippenham

Contents

Chapter 1

SS *Voco*

AFTER completing twenty-two months of a two year contract serving as 3rd Mate on the MV *Penrith Castle*, a twin
screw motor ship, I arrived in Liverpool on 22 August 1939.
This vessel was engaged in trading to ports around the world
commencing in New York and ending in New York. As many
as twenty ports would be called at in each four-month trip
covering the Far East but excluding Europe. I had not been
home during this time, but this was normal for seafarers before
the war when the terms of agreement were for two years. I was
released at twenty-two months only because it was cheaper to
send me home from New York than it would have been two
months later when the vessel was somewhere in the Far East.

The trip from New York to Liverpool on the Cunard liner
Samaria took eight days and I found it very boring. I had
travelled on passenger ships before but only to join a vessel
abroad or to return to the UK, and I never sailed as part of the
crew. I never had any desire to serve on passenger vessels which
before the war seemed to me like great floating hotels. In those
days, when forging my career in tramp ships and world-wide
traders, I had circumnavigated the globe ten times by the time
I was twenty-two. This could never have been achieved on a

passenger vessel. Despite the more comfortable and easier life, with frequent home visits, I did not consider this as my idea of 'going to sea'. I had travelled before on passenger ships but only when going to join a vessel in the USA or returning after completing a contract. There were also transfers from one ship to another when abroad. I was always bored. I could never appreciate the enthusiasm of some of my fellow passengers who took it upon themselves to act as unelected organisers of deck sports and games. Going outward I would naturally be a little sad at having to leave my family and friends for a long time by my own free will whilst at the same time I would look forward to the challenge ahead and the prospect of seeing more of the world.

Coming back the trip couldn't be over quickly enough and in your elated state you could be apt to part with some of your hard earned savings to the saloon barman. This could certainly curtail your time spent ashore, for there was no paid leave at that time, but it was better than shuffleboard and being organised. My only concern was to get home as quickly as possible, have a break and then enrol in the Nautical College to study, then sit examinations, for my 1st Mate's Certificate.

My well-laid plans for a rest and then study were to no avail for as history will show, on 3 September 1939 we declared war on Germany. I had been at home for just eleven days. The College was due to open again after the summer recess but did not do so. I could not afford to remain at home for too long doing nothing at all. If I was studying I was entitled to draw a small sum from the unemployment office for a limited time. Being a registered and career seafarer I could not be called up. Like so many young men of that time I had this strong feeling of patriotism and, since the country was at war, I would better serve it by going back to sea.

It was these circumstances that led me just nine days later to sign on the tanker *Voco* of Socony Vacuum Oil Company. She was engaged in carrying the company's lubricating oil products from refineries on the east coast of America to UK installations in Birkenhead, the River Thames and Manchester. The *Voco* was a vessel of about 4,000 gross tons and the registered owners were the Standard Transportation Company of Hong Kong.

I joined the *Voco* in Birkenhead as she was just completing discharging her last cargo. She was a very smart looking vessel but her livery was to me quite unusual. Most companies had their own colour schemes, for hull, masts, deck housing and funnel, and could be distinguished by these characteristics. The deck housing on the *Voco* was painted a dark red and this was covered with varnish to protect it from the salt spray encountered on her Atlantic voyages. The tank hatches and lids, of which there were many, were painted green. The funnel was black with a white 'V' on either side. Before sailing every inch of outside paintwork and all brasswork, including telegraphs, binnacle and ship's regulation bell, had to be painted over with Admiralty grey. Many famous companies would now lose their identity. Before, at sea or in port, ships could be recognised by their livery as to which company they belonged to, but except for the number of funnels and masts and size, all ships would now look very much alike. Regular liner cargo vessels and tramp ships all the same wrapped in grey.

We eventually sailed from Birkenhead for the oil port of Bayonne in New Jersey. In these early days we were able to go south down St George's Channel and then due west out into the

North Atlantic. An escort of frigates took us part of the way across until they had to return in order to re-fuel. From then we just set course for our final destination. This was made easier by the fact that we had on board a gyro compass which was quite new to me at this time. The voyage was free from attack but there was always the alertness and awareness that it could happen at any time. Keeping station in company with a limited number of ships was, of course, new to everyone, except perhaps to a few older hands who may have been at sea towards the end of the 1914–18 War. It didn't seem too difficult but bore no resemblance to conditions in the larger convoys which were to follow with the constant threat of attack from submarine, surface raider and, when in range, enemy aircraft.

I had sailed as 3rd Mate of a tanker for eleven months in 1937. She only carried spirit which could be quickly loaded and discharged; consequently the time spent in port was very short. Various grades of lubricating oil were loaded into many different tanks and the life of the tanker officer was much more leisurely on the *Voco*. We also loaded at two other ports after completion in Bayonne. They were Paulsboro and Chester in Delaware Bay about 180 sea miles away.

People I met were not very interested in knowing that we had come from and would return to a war zone. Not a lot was happening in Britain at the time. Almost all the action was at sea. There was one unpleasant incident which occurred when we were in Bayonne. I had the night off and decided to take the ferry and go across to Manhattan to visit some friends of mine. New York had been my home port for some years before the war and after saying goodbye to me about six weeks ago they would be surprised to see me again so soon. I had not been in contact to say I was coming and upon arrival at their apartment found that they were out. It was a long way back to Bayonne and, who knows, I might never be here again, so I decided to call back a little later. To while away the time I went into a nearby bar and ordered a beer. After being served and given my change the bartender said, 'If I were you I would drink that and go out.' I didn't at first understand why but on looking over my shoulder saw a group of men looking at me and making hostile remarks. It was obvious that I was not welcome, so I did the sensible thing and went out. Later, in the company of my friends, I learned that this particular bar was frequented by the Irish community who were anti-British. They must have heard my English accent. The 'Irish Question' as we referred to it in 1993 has been in evidence for a long time. I remember small explosive devices being put into post or pillar boxes in London and other cities by activists. I had left the bar without any trouble but thought afterwards what nonsense it all was. I was hurt to think that I was probably more Irish than anyone on the premises and perhaps more Irish than their parents. At least I was first generation born in Liverpool.

The homeward voyage across the Atlantic was pretty much the same as the outward one. We were now bound for Manchester and were met by our escorting frigates somewhere south of Iceland, thus giving the Channel approaches a wide berth. We had scares but no direct attack, but during my time on the *Voco* thirty-two ships had been sunk. These were early days; it was only the second week in November 1939.

On arrival at Eastham Locks before proceeding up the Manchester Ship Canal there were now clear signs that there was a war on. Machine gun and anti-aircraft emplacements had been erected on the approaches to the locks and inside on the canal banks. I made inquiries and found that the College had re-opened so I decided that after tying-up in Manchester I would leave and revert to my original plan to study for the next grade. I had made my first crossing of the Atlantic in war time and had come back unscathed. There were many more to follow but surely they would be more hazardous.

Chapter 2

SS *Lancaster Castle*

A FTER obtaining my 1st Mate's certificate I returned to my old company and was appointed 2nd Mate of the SS *Lancaster Castle*. This was one more step up the ladder of my seafaring career which started late in 1930 when I sailed as a deck boy on a two-mast topsail schooner. I then served four years as an apprentice and two years as 3rd Mate on ocean-going cargo and tanker vessels.

The SS *Lancaster Castle*, a vessel of 5,171 gross tons, had been built in 1937. She was what you might call a modern tramp ship and had roamed around the world before the outbreak of the war. The accommodation on board was vastly superior to that of the tramp ships in which I had served my time. I had had a short spell on an earlier vessel of the same name but she was no longer in the fleet and I would think had been scrapped. Despite these improvements she was still a steamship, using coal as fuel to feed the boilers.

I was now the 2nd Mate with specific duties allocated to this rank. The most important of these was that on this size of ship I was the navigating officer responsible for charts etc. I now kept the 12–4 a.m. and p.m. watches and was on the bridge in the forenoon to take sights and, with other officers, determine the ship's position. I also had a different station when entering or leaving port. As 3rd Mate my station had been on the bridge, recording engine movements and relaying instructions. Now I was in charge of the stern mooring and unmooring.

I suppose it could be said that I should have stayed at sea and not taken time off to attend college and sit an examination for a higher grade certificate. A period of study was necessary before taking the examination set by the Board of Trade or the Ministry of Transport. As the war went on the losses in Merchant Navy personnel increased and grades right up to Master Mariner would have to be obtained in order to keep the service afloat.

The whole of my time on the *Lancaster Castle* was spent in trans-Atlantic voyages to the USA and Canada, bringing back all types of war equipment: tanks, vehicles, etc., plus essential foodstuffs. This was Britain's lifeline. All voyages were fraught with danger as the sinkings increased and we were always on constant alert. Some voyages were more eventful than others.

After a few successful crossings of the Atlantic the *Lancaster Castle* could be called a 'regular' and on eastward crossings, when met by the British escort vessels, one destroyer, not very modern but also a 'regular', seemed to note that we were in the particular convoy he was out to protect. This vessel made a point of steaming down the column in which we were stationed, blew its siren and gave us a wave. It was like 'nice to see you again, glad you are still around (or afloat)'. It was most reassuring.

After one hazardous and exciting voyage we had to spend a few days in dry dock in Liverpool for minor repairs. The parents of one of the apprentices on board kept a small hotel in

North Wales called the Pwllgwyn; it lay between Mold and Denbigh. The Mate, 2nd Mate (myself) and the 2nd Engineer were invited to spend a few days there. This was a very kind gesture on their part and was made so that we could have a quiet rest in the countryside away from the tensions of the North Atlantic, and out of Liverpool, which was being regularly bombed. The hotel was on the main road near the village of Caerwys and stood alone. There was hardly any passing traffic, no doubt because of the strict petrol rationing. Travelling was done by rail and every village had its own station. The one at Caerwys was some distance from the hotel so we strolled leisurely along enjoying the scenery and the quietness. After settling in we enjoyed a few drinks and an excellent meal then decided to turn in early and get some of the prescribed rest.

I think it was the Mate who suggested after breakfast the next morning that we went for a nice healthy walk. This is something sailors are not very used to. Opposite the hotel there were hills of beautiful green pastureland. They were just hills but looked like mountains to us. It was our intention to climb to the top of the summit of the hill right ahead. The further we went the further the top seemed to be. A remark from the Mate suddenly changed everything. He looked at his watch and said, 'It's half past eleven, they must be open by now.' It was then about-turn and full speed ahead on both legs. Going downhill was like having the tide with you and soon three thirsty mariners were berthed in the saloon bar of the Pwllgwyn Hotel. From then on, I am afraid it became an indulgence in the bottle or the pump. It wasn't fresh air we needed. There was plenty of that on the oceans. This sort of break didn't improve our physical condition very much at all but I can assure you that after five days when we again went out into the Atlantic we were mentally refreshed beyond all measure and ready for any eventuality.

* * *

Much has been written by historians and others about this epic convoy No. HX84 which was attacked in mid-Atlantic by the German battleship *Admiral Scheer*. The convoy had just one escort, an armed merchant cruiser, the *Jervis Bay*, whose peace-time role was the carriage of passengers to and from Australia. The attack commenced at 5.00 p.m. on 5 November 1940. Immediately the *Admiral Scheer* approached the convoy the *Jervis Bay* steamed out from her position in the middle of the leading column. The bravery of Captain Fogarty Fegan and his crew will be remembered by all who escaped through his action. Had he not steamed towards the raider, thus drawing his fire, whilst at the same time giving orders to the convoy to scatter and make smoke to try and conceal ourselves, and had it not been 5.00 p.m. in November with the light fading, the whole of the convoy would have been annihilated. As it was, six ships only were sunk. Captain Fegan was awarded the Victoria Cross posthumously. He steamed out of the convoy to certain death. As the 2nd Officer of the *Lancaster Castle*, one of the vessels which escaped, I would like to record my own memories of this famous voyage.

The *Lancaster Castle* had loaded a full cargo of grain in Three Rivers in the St. Lawrence River, Canada, and was bound for Grangemouth in the Firth of Forth via Loch Ewe in west Scotland. We sailed from Three Rivers on the morning of 25 October and proceeded to Sydney, Cape Breton to join up with other vessels bound for the UK. The main convoy had left Halifax, Nova Scotia and we rendezvoused with them according to plan. We had sailed from Sydney on 29 October and steamed in a general easterly direction until the afternoon of the 31st, and had been steaming at just over 7 knots. At noon on 1st November we were in position 45°27'N 49°01'W. The true course made good over the previous twenty-four hours was N54E. I have no record of any alterations of course during the day in my Sight Book. We continued steering in a north-easterly direction and our position at noon on 5 November was 52°30'N 33°37'W and our speed over the previous twenty-four hours had been 8.76 knots. This position was near enough right in the middle of the North Atlantic. The weather was wind north-east 4, moderate sea and swell, cloudy and clear.

I have in my possession my original Sight Book, written in pencil, which gives daily positions, courses, speed, weather and so on throughout the whole of this voyage and many other Atlantic passages during the time when I was serving as 2nd Mate, the navigating officer.

I took over the bridge watch at noon and dealt with the relaying of our noon position as we had calculated it, to all other vessels. This was done by flying our position in international code flags from the foremast. Our position in the convoy was the rear ship in column one. There were thirty-eight ships in all, and I think we were in rows of six. Various alterations of speed had to be made to maintain station but all in all it was an uneventful watch. I was relieved at 4.00 p.m. by the Chief Officer and after telling him the course and speed required and the present engine revs to indicate whether we were gaining or falling back on the vessel ahead, we both took a careful scan of the horizon through our binoculars. There was nothing in sight other than our convoy so I went down below.

It was usual on this class of vessel for the evening meal to commence at 17.00 hours or 5.00 p.m. I was in the saloon and was about to attack a strange dish, one I had not had before and have no wish to have again, when gun-fire was heard. Those of us in the saloon at the time rushed up to the bridge. The raider was approaching from the north-west. When first seen on the horizon it was thought that we had been given another more powerful escort which was now joining up with us. This idea was soon dispelled when he opened fire and the *Jervis Bay* steamed out to meet him. The raider had 11″ guns and far superior armament to the *Jervis Bay* which was hit repeatedly and went on fire; but those on board, who must have known their fate, kept on firing until the end.

As 2nd Mate I was also the Gunnery Officer. All alarms had been sounded and the crew were at their station on the 4″ gun platform on the poop deck. Before running aft I nipped into my cabin to grab a piece of cotton wool to stuff in my ears. I hated the noise and always had the cotton wool with me when we had gun practice. By this time we had received orders to scatter so the initial move would be away from the action which, as we were steering north-east, meant a large alteration to starboard, thus leaving us as one of the nearest ships to the enemy. I think we were the first merchant ship to open fire and we managed to get quite a few 4″ shells away but I'm afraid hits were not possible. The raider could have been five miles away. It was hard to judge. It seemed that after a while the raider got fed up with our barking like a Yorkshire terrier snapping at an Alsatian so he turned his secondary armaments towards us, presumably 6″, and fired a salvo. It was like saying, 'Keep quiet, I will deal with you later.' We were very fortunate that he missed us and hit the vessel ahead which I don't think had been annoying him. Darkness was now closing in and we could do no more than try and make our escape. The Captain of the *Lancaster Castle*, Captain Hugh Williams, called his officers together on the bridge and it was decided that every time we saw a gun flash we would turn our stern to it and make as much speed as possible away from it. The weather was still moderate. I mention Captain Williams because I had sailed under him for a long time, first as an apprentice when he was Mate then as 3rd Mate and 2nd Mate when he was in command on different vessels. He was a very experienced master, respected by all. He was tragically lost when his vessel, our sister ship the *Lowther Castle*, was torpedoed off Bear Island when in a Russian convoy in 1942.

Ships were now steaming in all directions and alterations of course were many. We were completely blacked out and the night was dark. There were some near misses but no collisions. One ship came so close to us going in the opposite direction that we could hear them shouting to us as she slid down our starboard side. Looming out of the darkness, she was a much larger vessel which I thought could be the *Rangatiki*.

When daylight came we found ourselves alone. The Master decided to steam due north. This we did until noon on the 6th, our position then being 55°43′N, 33°43′W. This was a dead reckoning position. From here we set course to pass north of Ireland to the Firth of Clyde, our nearest safe haven. Loch Ewe would have to wait. The weather then deteriorated and we had Force 8 ESE gales. These moderated for a while on the 8th and then backed to the west and increased to Force 9 NW.

We arrived in Rothesay Bay at 16.45 on 11 November. This was Armistice Day and it was fitting that we had found a peaceful anchorage in which to rest a while. November 5th, the evening of the attack, was of course Bonfire Night, and we had our own firework display made by gun flashes and vessels catching fire. From the time of the attack it had taken us six days to reach Rothesay Bay and it was remarkable that we had been alone for six days in some of the most U-Boat infested areas for that time. Admiralty records show that 73 ships were lost in the month of November 1940, and by the end of 1940 1,200 ships had been sunk, but we had sailed 1,200 miles to safety, unescorted, after escaping from the *Admiral Scheer*. One afternoon when I was on watch we saw an aircraft approaching from ahead. Was it one of ours or not? We had in the Chart Room sheets of silhouettes of all enemy and Allied aircraft operating at that time. It wasn't until he peeled off that I was able to recognise the type, and sufficient to say that it was one of ours. Tension was relieved and we would be reported as being safe at least up till then. We were well clear of the raider the next day, for the Admiralty knew of the events and would surely be dispatching heavily armed naval craft to engage her. The enemy would not have attempted to come further north.

Looking back on that evening of 5 November one memory sticks very clearly in my mind. This was the manning of the 4″ gun. It was situated on top of the poop deck house, with the magazine in the small tonnage hatch just forward of the housing. It was the ship's carpenter's job to pass shells out of the locker and they were then passed up to the main deck via a ladder, then up another ladder to the gun platform. The human chain passing up the ammunition was made up of apprentices plus cabin, messroom and galley boys. The eldest could not have been more than 17½ and some were much younger. You could be proud of

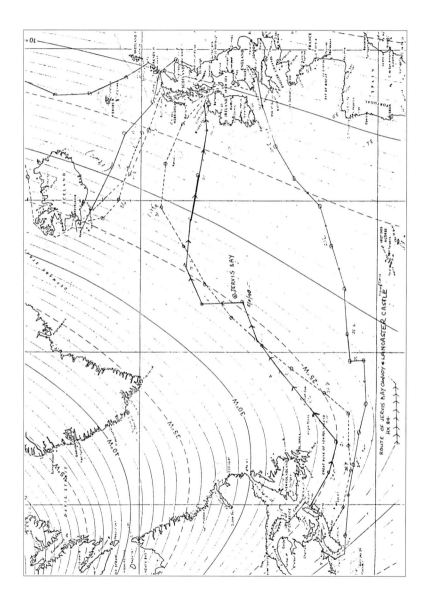

these young men, for men they were. At this stage it seemed very unlikely that any of the vessels in the convoy could avoid being sunk or damaged, yet these youngsters behaved magnificently. My own thoughts at the time were quite strange. I had been in dangerous situations before and had seen other vessels sunk in convoy but I knew it was never going to happen to me. I was going to survive the war all right. But this was something different. It was not an unannounced explosion of a U-Boat torpedo but as if I was going to be picked off. After the initial feeling of fear I felt elated, almost exultant, and the adrenalin flowed. A sobering thought was: I wonder if my mother will know how I died. There were four of us brothers at sea and I know she was constantly thinking about us and praying. To have four sons at sea throughout the war sailing in all theatres and all coming home safely at the end was remarkable. One mother's prayers were answered.

After a few days in the Clyde estuary and then being re-routed we arrived in Methil in the Firth of Forth, then sailed on to Grangemouth to discharge our much needed grain cargo. The official Admiralty communiqué stated that all but nine of the ships attacked in the convoy had escaped and named twenty-four ships as having arrived in port. It also stated that it was possible that other vessels still missing could eventually arrive back safely. This proved to be true as eventually we learned that only six vessels had actually been lost out of a total of thirty-eight. Sixty-five survivors from the *Jervis Bay* were picked up by a merchant ship which I believe was Swedish and she proceeded westwards to the USA or Canada.

This communiqué was broadcast to the nation; both my parents and the girl whom I later married heard it and knew that

...e

...chland

another
a port how
...uiser of the
class was

...Orders were given for the convoy
to scatter, and the Jervis Bay faced
the raider, guns blazing," he said.

"Although out-gunned, she kept
the warship at bay as the ships in
convoy made off.

"The Jervis Bay was badly
damaged with the first few shots
from the raider and quickly took fire.

"She was seen to be in a sinking
condition, but although her decks
were awash her guns still roared."

GREAT GALLANTRY

The British captain said: "The
raider's shooting was accurate and
regular, often five shells being fired
in one group. The raider was then
about eight miles off, and I estimated
that the salvoes were from 11-inch
guns.

"The raider had everything in her
favour. Our escort ship, the Jervis
Bay, acted with great courage and
gallantry.

"She sailed out to meet the German ships, while the other ships were
ordered to scatter in the gathering
dusk.

"Those on board the Jervis Bay
must have known what their fate
would be but they went on firing
their guns as long as they could.

"The German ship had, however,
an overwhelming mass of guns
trained on her, and the unequal
contest ended with the gallant
British ship going up in flames.

"Her end was in keeping with the
glorious traditions.

"As we scurried off to the safety
of the darkening night, we heard
more guns flash, and presumed the
warship was attacking other members
of the convoy.

"We owe our lives to the gallant
fellows on the Jervis Bay "

OFFICIAL STORY

Here is the Admiralty communique,
issued late last night:—

It can now be stated with certainty
that all except nine of the ships in
the convoy attacked by an enemy
surface raider on the night of November 5, escaped.

The convoy consisted of 38 ships.

One of the ships had dropped
astern.

It will be remembered that the
German High Command announced
that the whole of this convoy had
been destroyed.

It is possible that some of the ships
still missing may be safe.

That nearly three-quarters of this
large convoy escaped destruction at
the hands of the powerful German
raider was due to the high degree of
efficiency shown by the captains of
the merchant vessels in scattering
and making use of smoke, and to the

very gallant action of the armed
merchant cruiser H.M.S Jervis Bay
(Acting-Captain E. S. F. Fegen, R.N.),
which was escorting the convoy.

Full details of this action are not
yet available, but it is known that
H.M.S. Jervis Bay steered for the
enemy and engaged her with greatly
inferior armament.

This enabled the majority of the
ships in the convoy to make good
their escape.

BURNING FURIOUSLY

H.M.S. Jervis Bay continued to
engage the enemy after she had been
severely hit and was burning
furiously.

Nearly two hours after the
beginning of the engagement, an
explosion was seen to take place on
board H.M.S. Jervis Bay, and it is
regretted that she must be considered
as lost.

It is known that 65 survivors of
H.M.S. Jervis Bay are on board a
merchant ship. The next of kin of
casualties will be informed as soon
as facts can be ascertained.

The following 24 ships of this
convoy have now arrived in port:—
Orodona, Andalusian, Cornish City,
Empire Penguin, James F. Maguire,
Danae II, Castilian, Briarwood, Varoy,
Athel Templar, Lancaster Castle, Dan
Y. Bryn, Athel Empress, Oil Reliance,
Solfonn, Hjalmar Wesse, Emile
Francqui, Persier, Delhi, Rangitiki,
Anna Bulgari, Delphonula, Cordelia,
Pacific Enterprise.

The Jervis Bay, in peace time, was
an Australian Commonwealth liner
and had a crew of 15 officers and
174 men.

In June, 1928, eight stowaways tried
to cause a mutiny among the crew
and to set fire to the ship. They
were put under hatches and guarded
by a posse of volunteer guards from
among the passengers.

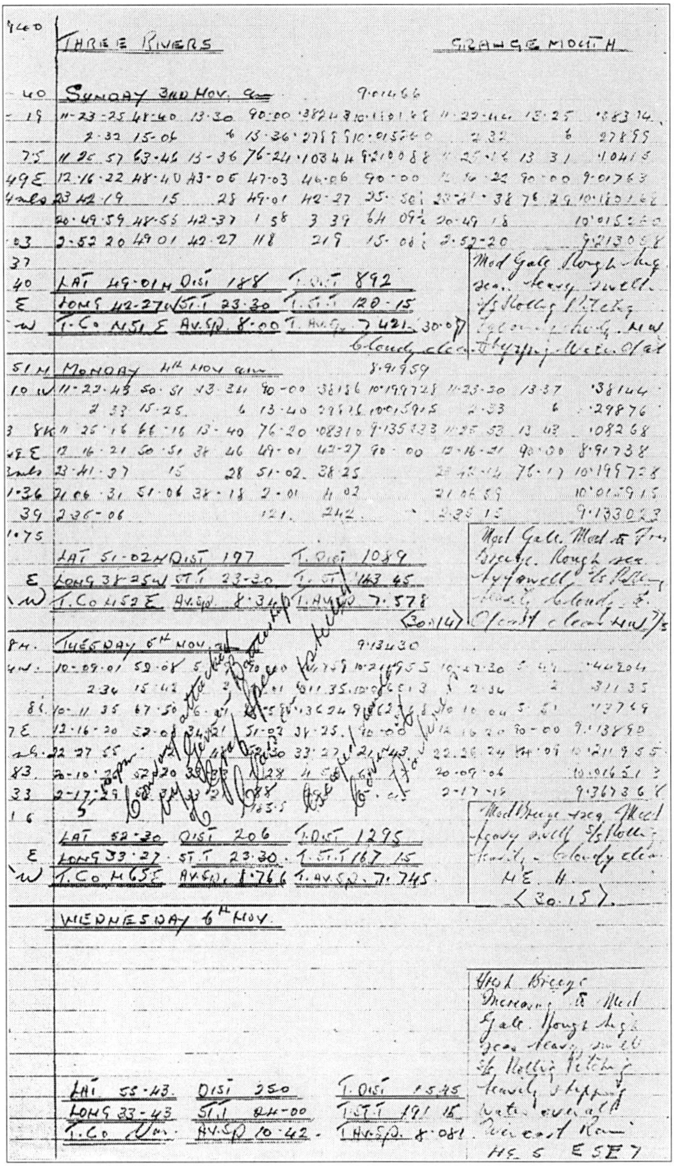
THREE RIVERS GRANGEMOUTH

SUNDAY 3RD NOV.

LAT 49·01N DIST 188 T. DIST 892

LONG 42·27W ST.T 23·30 T.S.T 120·15

T.CO N51E AV.SP. 8·00 T. AV.SP. 7·421

MONDAY 4th NOV

LAT 51·02N DIST 197 T. DIST 1089

LONG 38·25W ST.T 23·30 T.S.T 143 45

T.CO N52E AV.SP. 8·34 T.AV.SP. 7·578

TUESDAY 5th NOV

LAT 52·30 DIST 206 T.DIST 1295

LONG 33·27 ST.T 23·30 T.S.T 167 15

T.CO N65E AV.SP. 8·766 T.AV.SP. 7·745

WEDNESDAY 6th NOV.

LAT 55·43 DIST 250 T.DIST 1545

LONG 33·43 ST.T 24·00 T.S.T 191 15

T.CO Dr. AV.SP. 10·42 T.AV.SP. 8·081

Author's Sight Book.

I was safe, at least up to that time. The German High Command however announced that the whole of this convoy had been destroyed. It was the practice up to this time for the BBC to report losses at sea and to name vessels, but this was the last time that this occurred. Losses were high and it was imprudent to fuel the enemy's propaganda machine. Secrecy then became the order of the day. It was not until we were safely in port that we knew the name of the surface raider which had attacked the convoy. I had scrawled across the entries in my Sight Book: '5.10 p.m. Convoy attacked by German battleship of Graf Spee class. Escaped under cover of darkness'. We now knew it was the *Admiral Scheer*.

We had been in company with the *Jervis Bay* before but in very different circumstances. We had sailed light ship across the Atlantic from Barry, South Wales, to St. John, New Brunswick to load a full cargo of timber. Unfortunately we suffered rudder damage when on passage. After a diver's examination it was found that we would need to go to dry dock for repairs. The dry dock was occupied at this time by the *Jervis Bay* which was undergoing surveys or some sort of modification and we had to wait quite some time before she was re-floated. During this time the crews of both vessels became friendly. Who could have foreseen that a couple of months later we would be together again in such tragic circumstances? The dockside had been piled high with 45-gallon drums which were empty and sealed. We heard that they were to be stowed in the holds of the *Jervis Bay*, presumably to give her extra buoyancy. This may have been an advantage had she been struck, say, by a solitary torpedo, but was to no avail when being bombarded by a craft such as the *Admiral Scheer*.

In recent years I have been asked many questions by an American historian about this convoy, two of which were, 'Did you know what happened to the other vessels which escaped? Did you ever meet any of the crew?' To answer: apart from the famous voyage home of the *San Demetrio* which was made into a film, I have no idea what happened to them at that time. We had arrived safely. Where the others ended up, which port and which date, I never thought about. After discharge in Grangemouth we were bound back across the North Atlantic and that was our main concern.

A volume published by Her Majesty's Stationery Office entitled *British Vessels Lost at Sea 1939–1945* gives details of every vessel lost or damaged.

At the time, and particularly after our safe arrival in port, I did not give much consideration to the fact that this convoy of thirty-eight ships was protected by just one AMC armed merchant cruiser, an ex-passenger vessel. I have wondered since how she could have dealt with a submarine attack.

Whenever Bonfire Night comes around I think of 5 November 1940 and my lucky escape. Had I not rushed onto the bridge I quite possibly would have eaten that strange dish of Tripe Fritters.

* * *

During my time on the *Lancaster Castle* I made seven voyages across the Atlantic to ports in the USA and Canada and one voyage to Cuba. This meant fourteen crossings, seven outward and seven homeward. We sailed in ballast from east coast ports, Bristol Channel ports, the Thames and the Mersey. The return cargoes consisted of war supplies such as tanks, vehicles and ammunitions and essential foods such as grain and sugar. All voyages were fraught with danger. There was the ever present threat of enemy U-Boat attack and in home waters attack from the air. We were on constant alert at all times. Some voyages were more eventful than others; none was uneventful. Every voyage was different, just as every peace-time voyage was different. Even on a regular run no two voyages could ever be the same. They obviously took much longer than peace-time voyages, because of the convoy system and the routes taken to avoid U-Boats and later the wolf packs. Some Atlantic crossings took us just south of Iceland and about 130 miles off the southern tip of Greenland. A normal voyage, say from London to Halifax, Nova Scotia, would take a vessel of this class 10½ days in fair weather. The distance is 2,635 miles from the Thames through the English Channel, then direct to Halifax. I made one voyage on the *Lancaster Castle* between the same ports and it took us twenty days. We did not, of course, sail down the English Channel but up the North Sea to Methil in the Firth of Forth, then in another convoy around the north of Scotland to Loch Ewe, where the Atlantic Convoy was formed. The route was changed many times during passage, as directed by the Commodore. On this particular voyage we steamed 3,784 miles between London and Halifax.

During these long voyages some sort of normal shipboard life had to go on. There was work to be done on deck, for ships were still maintained in a clean and efficient condition. There was ever this feeling of pride in your vessel and the overhauling of machinery and equipment went on as usual. This particular maintenance work was vital if using ship's gear to discharge the

Jones (3rd Engineer); Author; Captain Williams; Hedgecock (4th Engineer); Leadley (2/RO).

cargo, and inspections and drills were held regularly. What to do with the limited leisure time was a problem.

Being aware that disaster could strike at any time didn't easily help you to relax. We were fortunate on the *Lancaster Castle* in that we all got on well together; some of us had been shipmates on other vessels of the Fleet, and during the whole of my time on this ship I think we only changed one officer. There were eleven officers on board as follows: Chief, 2nd and 3rd Deck or Navigating Officers; Chief, 2nd, 3rd and 4th Engineer Officers; 1st, 2nd and 3rd Radio Officers; and of course the Captain himself. I think it was the 1st Radio Officer who thought of it first, then, together with others, devised a plan to form our own social club on board. This was to be called the '10.30 Club', as meetings were to take place every Sunday morning at this hour.

We already had a meeting place, the Engineers' messroom. Before the war, deck officers and engineers dined separately except for the Chief Engineer, who dined with the navigators and the Captain. Now we were all as one in the officers' saloon. This left the Engineers' messroom vacant. It wasn't a large room but it was sufficient for our activities. Rules were drawn up and a Rule Book printed and given to each member, including the Captain. A medallion was struck of brass, made by the engineers, which was about the size of the present £1 coin; stamped on it were the figures '10.30'. The Headquarters was known as 'The Crank and Compass' and it was forbidden for any member to enter without his membership medallion. To do so could mean a challenge to produce it and failure to do so meant an instant fine. A dartboard was acquired in some port and later from some second-hand shop an old fashioned 'potty', which was expertly covered with silver paper and became the cup awarded to the darts champion. A rotary system for chairman was drawn up and the person in the chair was responsible for the minutes and the supply of all refreshments for those present. At sea of course we could never have all eleven members present at one time as some were on watch, but if it was convenient they would be relieved if only to put in a brief appearance and register. Shown against the names of Sloan, McBrearty and Williams in the list of members are the letters CCC. This stands for the Crank and Compass Cross, awarded with all ceremony to those members for their action when they disposed of an incendiary device on a bus in Swansea during an air-raid. Not many receive cardboard medals.

In port it was a strict rule that all members attended or were fined for non-attendance. It was all done in a light-hearted manner with lots of laughs and phoney solemnity. It provided a great relief from the tensions of the day. Even when ashore a member had always to be in possession of his 10.30 Club medallion. If when in a bar ashore another member came in, he could be challenged to produce his identity coin. Anyone without it would have to pay for the drinks. Fines which accrued during meetings and elsewhere were put into the Treasurer's bank (his pocket) and when sufficient funds were available an extraordinary meeting would be called to dispose of them. The 'Club' became quite well known and in various ports shore personnel, agents for example, were made honorary members.

The most distinguished member of the 10.30 Club was the Hon Sir Herbert Meade-Fetherstonhaugh, CCVO, CB, DSO. He was made a member when he became part of the ship's company. On a voyage from Liverpool to New York via Halifax

"10.30 Club"
Official Membership List.

Brother	Craigie. (Founder)
"	Williams C.C.C.
"	Rouffenac.
"	Jones.
"	Wray.
"	White.
"	Gowland.
"	Sloan C.C.C.
"	Ruxton. (Office)
"	Martin. (Office)
"	Kelly. (Captain)
Sister	Craigie.
Brother	Midgeley.
Sister	Midgeley.
Brother	Roxborough.
"	Barlow.
Sister	Whatley. H. (N.O. La.)
"	Whatley. D. (N.O. La.)
Brother	Williams. (Captain)
"	Mc Brearty C.C.C.
"	Leadley.
"	Jones.
"	Johnson.
"	Admiral The Hon., Sir Herbert. Meade–Fetherstonhaugh C.C.V.O., C.B., D.S.O.
"	Hedgecock.
Sister	Williams.
"	Johnson.
Brother	Hooper.

Note: The Secretary regrets that the official liste of members of the "10.30 Club" (BRANCH) S.S. "Lowther Castle" is not available at the time of going to print.

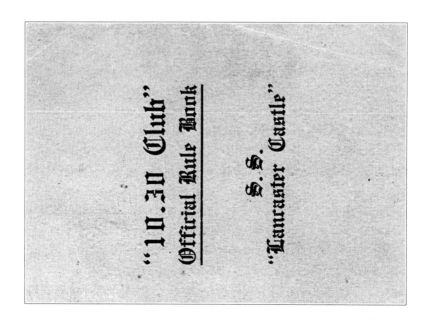

"10.30 Club"

Official Rule Book

S. S.

"Lancaster Castle"

the *Lancaster Castle* was assigned the role of Commodore Ship. This meant that we would take up position in the centre of the front line and would have on board the Convoy Commodore who would direct operations in liaison with the senior officer of the naval escort. At this time most of the Commodores of Atlantic convoys were high ranking retired Royal Naval officers who had volunteered, or even demanded, to be brought back into service to do all that they could to help to win the Battle of the Atlantic.

I am not sure why we were chosen to be the leader but it was possibly because we were the most suitable vessel of those assembled in Liverpool to accommodate him. The *Lancaster Castle* was a typical modern tramp steamer built a couple of years before the war. Our big advantage was that we had a very fine spare cabin adjacent to the officers' saloon. It had very modern conveniences for vessels of the time, with running water and a shower. And so Admiral Sir Herbert Meade-Fetherstonhaugh came on board the evening before departure.

I was the Navigating Officer and as such was responsible for plotting the courses as instructed. After forming up and leaving Liverpool Bay we ran into dense fog. We were scheduled to rendezvous with another section of the convoy which had sailed from the Firth of Clyde. Our sort of old-fashioned navigation in these conditions involved using the mechanical log aft and paying strict attention to wind and weather and more particularly to the strength and direction of the tide. There was no radar in those days. The weather later cleared up and we arrived at the appointed position almost right on time. The Admiral was pleased with our efforts and said so. I don't suppose he had sailed on a merchant ship before and might have been a little apprehensive of our ability. Perhaps he did not know that we were professional navigators who did this job for a living and were trained to make every passage as short as possible with due regard to weather conditions and fuel consumption. This was essential in the commercial world. Now we had to make courses to pass north of Ireland and then sail westward across the Atlantic to Halifax.

I remember the Admiral as a splendid character who showed no pretensions of rank or position. He had a slight limp in one leg and wore a very old uniform jacket with a blue shirt and no cap. My watch was the lonely 12 to 4 and often after midnight he would appear on the bridge to assess weather conditions and the general position of the convoy. Over a mug of tea he would chat about many things. He was, I believe, at one time Admiral of the Fleet Mediterranean and would recall memories of his earlier days. He had been a junior officer on a British cruiser on the Far East station during the surrender of the garrison at Manila in the Philippines to the American Fleet. The British man of war was only in the area to observe the happenings. The Admiral's account of the battle was somewhat at variance with some historic accounts. He told me that at a pre-arranged signal the garrison fired a salvo at the American Fleet assembled in Manila Bay. This was met by instant counter-fire which brought about the immediate capitulation and surrender and so began the American occupation of the Philippine Islands.

Just before leaving Liverpool there was a report of a naval casualty somewhere off the French coast. It appears that two British destroyers were on patrol when one was sunk by the enemy. The other vessel returned to the scene and picked up some survivors. The Admiral was furious about this. He claimed that if he had his way the Commander of the second vessel should be court-martialled. He had jeopardised the safety of his own crew and could also have lost his own vessel. It was, he said, against Admiralty instructions. We also had orders that we were not to turn back during an attack to pick up survivors. (Later on in the war, when I was Chief Officer of a vessel in the Mediterranean, I did just that and picked up soldiers from a troop ship.)

I earned a pat on the back for my shooting ability one morning about halfway through our voyage. Certain vessels were ordered to drop astern and fire a live round at a target which consisted of a forty-gallon oil drum with a white flag attached. The drum had holes punched in it so it would eventually sink. I was in charge of the 4″ gun and when we took our turn I helped the range finder a bit by carefully checking my watch when the drum was thrown overboard. Knowing our speed through the water, I waited until I reckoned we had travelled a certain distance, then shouted, 'Fire!' Amazingly, we nearly hit the drum. All this was being observed through powerful binoculars from the bridge. Yes, he was well pleased with the exercise.

Being Commodore ship meant that officers on board knew all that was happening regarding alterations of course or speed and it was us who sent out the signal to the other vessels in the convoy, either by flag hoist or Aldis daylight signalling lamp. This was made easier as the Admiral had brought with him his own signalling staff consisting of a PO and two naval ratings. They were trained specifically for this sort of duty whereas on our own we would have to have replied to all signals by flag or lamp and to hoist daily positions with just one officer on the bridge with an apprentice to assist him. We were grateful to be relieved of this task.

We were sorry to see the Admiral leave and as he was drawing away from the ship's side with his staff in a launch he turned and waved us goodbye. I thought then of the last time we had chatted together in the middle of the night when he had invited me, should we both survive the war, to visit him at his country residence. You know the saying, 'Should you be in the area, don't fail to call.' This time I think he meant it. Whether he survived the war I do not know. After we had landed the Admiral in Halifax he would certainly after a brief rest have returned to the UK in charge of an eastern-bound convoy.

* * *

On this particular voyage we had another extra body on board, not connected with the war effort but because of it.

Just before sailing a dog was brought on board and we had instructions to look after it, feed it and deliver it to New York, where it would be collected. It was a beautiful animal, a Lakeland terrier, brown and black and smooth-haired. The Chief Officer appointed himself the dog's keeper and instead of it living in the kennel provided it spent almost all of the time in his cabin. He would take it 'walkies' up and down the main deck with a short length of boat lacing as a lead. He became very fond of the dog and didn't encourage anyone else to take part in the 'looking after' of the animal. It was obvious that the dog was very attached to him and would greet him with a great show of affection whenever he appeared. They were good companions. We assumed that the dog belonged to some important person, perhaps a diplomat, who had had to go hurriedly to the USA so that his pet had to be forwarded later.

We hadn't been in New York long before two men boarded bearing a note with instructions to collect the Chief Officer's dog, for that was what it was now called. We knew that it would have to go ashore and at one time it was suggested that we should hide it and say that it had been lost overboard. This would however have involved too many people, so parting with it it had to be. When the dog came to be carried away he started to create hell. He howled and howled and was very distressed. I'm sure he felt life was much better living with his foster master. The Mate didn't take too kindly to the situation either and was not very good company for the next couple of days.

* * *

This back and forth across the North Atlantic took us to many ports on the north-eastern coast of the USA and Canada. In the early days of the war we were treated with friendliness and sometimes sympathy in whichever port we arrived at. On a voyage from Milford Haven to New York we were attacked by enemy fighters soon after leaving the harbour and the starboard mid-ship accommodation was riddled with machine gun holes. There were no casualties and temporary repairs were soon effected as we were in a ballast condition. Had we been loaded and the hull had been hit we would have had a difficult job plugging holes in the hull.

On arriving in New York harbour we were met by dozens of small craft sailing around us and pointing to our guns and the improvised patches on the starboard accommodation. They would be seeing for the first time an armed merchant ship in her new livery sporting a 4″ gun aft. When ashore most people we met were friendly and would ask questions about how things were going in far off Europe. Of course, at this time the average American looked upon the conflict as a faraway war in which they would have no real interest and which could not possibly affect them. Or so they thought.

I had been in most of the Atlantic seaboard ports of the USA before the war, and one of the ports was Baltimore. On a voyage there in February 1941, ten months before the Japanese attack on Pearl Harbour, I expected a rather cool reception from the local inhabitants as I had formed an opinion before the war that Baltimore had a large proportion of its citizens who were of German origin. This was just my recollection from previous visits, but I am unable to vouch for it.

It was therefore with great surprise that one day, when loading our usual cargo of war supplies, a message was delivered on board inviting the officers and crew to a party. There were another couple of British ships in port at the time and they had the same invitation. There was more surprise and joy when we discovered that the party, plus entertainment, was to be held in a local brewery. The brewery, I seem to remember, was called Monsons or something sounding like that. Half the ship's company attended on one day and the other half on the following day. The party was arranged by the British Consul in conjunction with ex-British nationals living in Baltimore and, of course, with the co-operation of the management of the brewery, who offered their quite large canteen as the venue. They must have been on our side. We sat about six to a table with each ship's company remaining together. One person from each table was appointed barman. He didn't have to go and order drinks of different varieties for there was no bar as such but just a point where there was an endless supply of beer: no hard stuff but just two taps, one dispensing light beer, the other dark beer. There was a very fine and substantial buffet provided by the owner of a city restaurant who had emigrated to America from Rock Ferry, Wirral, Cheshire. There was live entertainment provided by artists from some of the local clubs and the British Consul himself gave a very fine rendering of 'Old Man River'. We were transported back to our various vessels in a very happy mood.

About ten years ago a very fine German film *Das Boot* (The Boat) was shown in serial form on the television. It showed the lives of the U-Boat commanders and their crews and was primarily about one particular U-Boat. We were shown how they lived in their cramped quarters on a long tour of duty starting in a French Atlantic port. There were screams of exultation when they made a 'kill' attacking some merchant vessel but also fear and bravery when they were being depth charged by an escorting destroyer. At one time they had to dive so deep that the hull plating began to leak. It seemed to me to be a truthful and dramatic account of the lives of our enemy in the Battle of the Atlantic.

I mention this film because it reminds me of the time when in convoy returning to the UK we were attacked in the middle of the night by a wolf pack of enemy U-Boats and a number of oil tankers were torpedoed. A similar scene was shown in *The Boat* when the U-Boat depicted had joined a wolf pack, a number of submarines working together which had shadowed the convoy and infiltrated it. It might have been taken during the actual action for it was exactly as I remembered it. Our position in the convoy was to the rear of one of the inner columns. It was a pitch-dark night and a tanker ahead of us had been hit and was now blazing furiously. The whole sky was lit up and we could see the silhouettes of other ships around us. The stricken vessel was now out of control and as we came upon her evasive action had to be taken to avoid running into her. I was the Officer of the Watch which was my usual one as 2nd Officer, keeping the midnight to 4 a.m. watch. I was not alone, however, for emergency signals had been sounded and I was joined on the bridge by the Captain and the other two deck officers. All the crew were now at emergency and action stations. We passed quite close to the burning vessels and could feel the heat from the raging flames. Worse still, we could hear the screams and shouts from the crew, some of whom were clustered on the poop deck as far away from the flames as they could get. It was no use jumping overboard for they would only have found themselves in a sea of burning oil. It was a sickening sight, and we could do nothing to help. It would have been sheer folly to attempt to turn around and go back in the hope of picking up survivors. To do so would have made our own vessel a sitting duck and it would have been impossible to get near enough with the sea ablaze. There were other vessels on fire and any attempt to go back would have caused confusion with vessels getting out of position and out of station in the convoy. As well as this it was the order of commanders that vessels should try to maintain their station and rescue attempts would be made only by the escorts.

In the film, the U-Boat eventually arrived back in her base port to find the band was playing and top brass on the quay to welcome them. Perhaps it was a fitting end that as they entered a lock a wave of British planes attacked with bombs and machine-gun fire and most, if not all, of the complement were killed. I have to say that they were shown as very brave men and I can agree with this after seeing their endurance under extremely hazardous conditions.

On one voyage from Halifax, Nova Scotia to Liverpool, we were five days out in the Atlantic when we heard of the loss of one of our largest naval vessels. The battle cruiser HMS *Hood* had been sunk by the German *Bismarck*. This was a severe blow, not only to our forces but to the morale of those engaged in the Battle of the Atlantic. Heads were lifted however by a speech broadcast by that splendid warrior and war leader, Winston Churchill. He could inspire you with his oration, by his tone of voice and his total conviction that we would eventually conquer and overthrow the evil Nazi régime. A few days later the *Bismarck* was destroyed.

* * *

We once loaded a full cargo in Canada of cut timber to be discharged in Portishead. At this time Portishead, situated below Avonmouth in the Bristol Channel, was not a large port. It had a power station with tall chimneys which could be seen when heading up the Channel. There was not a lot of quay space and I thought at the time that the *Lancaster Castle* was quite a big vessel to enter the port. Cargoes of timber were a necessary import. Buildings had to be repaired and people still needed furniture. We had loaded as much as possible using every available space. As deck officers, we were going up and down the hold ladders to make sure that this was so. A tight stow was necessary and in addition the decks were piled high with timber in accordance with BOT rules, which were just as strict then as they are today. They were called Timber Cargo Regulations and determined the height to which the deck cargo could be loaded and the size and type of lashings required to secure it. It took quite some time to discharge the cargo which could only be done in daylight working hours because of black-out regulations. Even daytime work was sometimes interrupted by air-raids or air-raid warnings when all shore personnel had to leave the ship and go to an air-raid shelter. Some of the dockers were quite elderly and would not have been doing this work in peace time, but the younger men were in the forces. One chap who I think was the eldest in the gang refused to go ashore. He just sat there on deck and when I asked him why he was not going to the shelter he replied in a very broad Somerset accent, 'I be old b——d I be; he can 'av I.'

There was a pub on the headland just below the harbour entrance which some of us frequented when not on duty. There were regular night raids over Bristol and Avonmouth. The landlord held a lottery in which you had to declare the exact time when the German night bombers would arrive. You placed your shilling bet on the huge cardboard clock face he had drawn. Depending on the number of customers on the premises and those willing to participate, the prize could be quite substantial. It was cash and the one shilling stake could buy two pints of beer. It was, of course, just fun and it showed the contempt they had for the Luftwaffe for no one thought of looking for a shelter.

On my way back one night with the Radio Officer, we decided to take a short cut across a field. When we had walked about half way the planes could be heard approaching. We had enjoyed our night ashore and the beverage that went along with it. Self-preservation was now uppermost in our minds and we crawled under a large hedgerow dividing the field. What protection the hedgerow would afford was not taken into consideration. After a few minutes all hell was let loose. Searchlights were criss-crossing the clear sky and on the other side of our 'bunker' an anti-aircraft battery was blasting away. My eardrums were throbbing so we made a run for it and raced towards the safety of our home, the ship. Strange, the things you do at times. Let's just say we were tired and needed a rest, so we sat down.

I did manage a trip home to Chester just for a weekend break when discharging was suspended. Most of the cargo was already ashore. General cargoes are usually kept in sheds alongside the quay until delivered to their various destinations, but timber cargoes end up being stacked away from the dock-side. It is amazing how much area is needed to stack a full cargo of timber from an average deep sea cargo vessel. When returning from my short visit home and approaching Portishead it seemed that the surrounding fields were covered with a huge carpet of wood.

I write about this cargo with the knowledge that it was about the best cargo you could carry whilst the sea battle raged in the Atlantic. Being loaded with timber gave a feeling of safety, like wearing a lifebelt; at least if you were torpedoed you would have a chance of getting off the vessel. A ship full of timber would take some sinking. All types of ship were sunk, but if hit there would be no fire; she could not just disappear, and I could be on my own kind of island. The brave men on the oil tankers had the worst deal of all. They could become engulfed in flames with even the sea around them burning with the spillage of oil. Any gas remaining in any of the tanks could explode with the impact of the torpedo.

By the summer of 1941, when we had made seven complete

voyages on the *Lancaster Castle*, it is recorded that the number of ships sunk during this period was 916. The total at the end of 1941 was 1361. Some of these voyages were more eventful than others, but none was uneventful. They were also getting longer because of the routes taken.

I was beginning to feel a little jaded and felt that I needed a short break. I requested to be relieved at the next terminal port of discharge. I considered myself to be lucky to have survived up to then without getting my feet wet, and was fortunate that on my last voyage we were bound for Liverpool. This suited me very well as my home was in Chester.

I was often asked by relations and friends before sailing to America or Canada if I would bring back items which were plentiful there and unrationed, such as clothing, perfume, silk stockings or nylons and booze. If married or doing a bit of old-fashioned courting you could be asked for more intimate female garments. I remember one voyage when the 2nd Mate dutifully obliged his current girl friend and bought a most expensive brand of perfume. Unfortunately he dropped it when going to his cabin. The smell lingered for days and days; we could hardly get rid of it. By the price of it I suppose one drop behind the ear would be sufficient to let others know what you were wearing.

If you agreed to participate in this 'bring me' game it was usually arranged that payment would be made upon delivery. I often thought, what if my ship was lost and the goodies with it? If I only brought myself back would anyone reimburse me for the money I had spent? How would they know if I had bought anything at all? The bottom of the North Atlantic must have been littered with bottles of perfume, packets of stockings, booze and other purchases which didn't made it across.

Chapter 3

SS *Lowther Castle*

I WAS not expecting to be recalled so soon but on 20 July 1941
I received a telegram from the owners of the *Lancaster Castle*
asking me to telephone them. This I did and was asked if I could
join the sister ship, the *Lowther Castle*, as 2nd Mate. She was
lying at anchor in Milford Haven fully laden with coal and
bound for Montevideo. She had loaded in Barry and was now
lying in the convoy assembly anchorage in Milford Haven.

To get to Milford Haven was quite a feat. Trains were few
and far between and those that were running were so full that
you were lucky if you could find floor space to sit down in the
corridor. I was travelling from Chester and had to change at
Shrewsbury. I was waiting some time on the platform with all
my clothes for another spell at sea which could last for many
months. Or, if I was unlucky, not very long at all. I also had my
badge of office with me: the small polished wooden box with
handle which contained my sextant. The tool of my trade, you
might say – a navigator.

Luck was with me at this stage for into the station came a train
with many carriages. I could see there were troops on board.
An announcement was made that this train was not to be
boarded; it was only for troops and was going to Milford

Haven. I immediately approached the Transport Officer and showed him my discharge papers and instructions for joining the *Lowther Castle*. I was given permission to board and found to my surprise an empty compartment. It was a long journey and I was able to stretch out. I had some funny looks when boarding the train for I was in civilian clothes. I was met at the station in Milford Haven and taken to the quay and was soon on my way to the anchorage by launch.

It took quite some time to reach the outer anchorage where a number of ships were lying awaiting sailing orders or perhaps just for me! I had no difficulty in finding the *Lowther Castle* as I had just spent sixteen months on her sister ship, and knew very well the look of her. I had all the gear with me needed for a long spell away, of course providing the enemy allowed it.

* * *

Sailing from Milford Haven we made our way slowly up the Irish Sea, rendezvousing with other sections from the Mersey and the Clyde to form the main convoy.

This voyage proved to be something different from the others I had made since war began. After a few days steaming in the Atlantic we were instructed to proceed independently. As we were stationed on the portside of the convoy we just peeled off when instructed to do so.

This was in a position roughly 49½°N 22½°W. From then on we headed in a south-west and then southerly direction to pass about fifty miles off the most eastern point of Brazil. We had steamed a distance of 7,036 miles at an average speed of 9.4 knots when we arrived on 30 August. We did not see any action on the way down but were always on constant alert. We steamed at night in complete darkness and lookouts were doubled at all times. Any navigation lights sighted were given a wide berth. The slightest wisp of smoke seen on the horizon meant an alteration of course to increase the distance between us. The U-Boats had not, up to now, operated in any strength on the east coast of South America as this was before Pearl Harbour and the entry of the USA into the war. There was, however, always the danger of attack by surface craft and armed raiders. The *Graf Spee* had operated successfully until trapped in Montevideo. I had vivid memories of my own experience when attacked by the *Admiral Scheer* when serving on the *Lancaster Castle* and was glad the *Graf Spee* had been put out of action during the famous Battle of the River Plate. We could see her scuttled hulk lying outside the breakwater when we were discharging in the harbour at anchor and she looked a sorry sight.

There were many fine organisations ashore offering succour, comfort and help to all seamen. The Mission to Seamen, the Apostleship of the Sea and other religious denominations had staff and buildings in most ports in the world. There was the watch ashore and countless women's organisations knitting furiously to keep us all warm in northern waters in winter. There was also the WVS, of which I shall be writing later. Of all the efforts made by the various organisations, the one made by the British residents of Montevideo was both marvellous and patriotic. There were all sorts of strange characters hanging around some neutral ports ready to latch on to the seamen and pump them for knowledge of the ship, destination or routes.

There was always the danger in neutral ports of enemy agents attempting to coerce or seduce any gullible seaman to obtain information and they could even disrupt the sailing of a vessel.

By the terms of the agreement signed by all members of the crew before commencing the voyage, shore leave could only be granted at the Master's discretion. This would be hard to impose after spending thirty or forty days at sea except in the case of an epidemic or revolution in the port visited, or when only stopping to replenish stores or fuel. All were advised to be most vigilant and the naval gunners on board of course wore their civilian clothes.

The British community in Montevideo found a way to combat this without curtailing the seaman's natural inclination to have a fling ashore after being cooped up for maybe weeks. They opened their own bar and called it 'The Liberty Inn'. The drinks were cheap and there were billiards and table-tennis. They would tell you in the Liberty Inn which shops they would advise you to use if you wished to go shopping, which transport or taxis to use, anything else you wanted they could direct you to places with no problems or spies. They would, of course, have preferred it if you stayed with company at the Inn. They also owned a sizeable motor launch and would bring crews ashore from ships lying at anchor. Sometimes it meant filling them up and taking them back. You never knew when in the Liberty Inn who the person serving you behind the bar was; he could be a director of the railways or a bank manager. They all took turns to do their bit.

We spent a week in Montevideo but as 2nd Mate I had to keep every other night on board. However, I did manage four trips in the Liberty Inn launch from the anchorages where we were discharging into lighters.

We left Montevideo on 7 September bound for Vitoria, a small port north of Rio in Brazil, to load iron ore for the UK. Raw

materials still had to be imported to maintain our own manufacturing output required for the war. The voyage took 4 days
22 hours and we steamed 1,287 miles. We were, of course, alone
and practised the usual precautions with strict double lookouts
and no lights. One dark night a ship bound south passed quite
close to us. She was also in darkness and must have been very
light draughted for I could hear the thrashing of her propeller.

Vitoria today is a modern port with excellent facilities to load
large vessels in record time. In September 1941, however, the
iron ore was dumped on the quayside and had to be loaded with
the ship's derricks lowering steel buckets into the holds. The
whole operation took ten days. Nowadays, much larger vessels
can load in hours at the modern terminal.

During our ten days in Vitoria we were received very well by
the local inhabitants and the Captain held a party on board for
the local dignitaries, which made us very popular. There was,
however, one dubious character roaming about. I had the impression that the port was not a busy one. There was no Liberty
Inn here so time ashore was spent in various bars and cafés
around the harbour area. This one person seemed always to try
and have a conversation with any of the crew he happened to
meet and went out of his way to be friendly. He was certainly
not Brazilian and I was very suspicious. I reported this to the
Master who informed the Shore Authorities. He had disappeared by the time we sailed.

Another vessel in the port was Danish with a Danish crew.
She had been there a long time, having been interned by the
Brazilians who were, at this time, a neutral country. Their vessel
had been immobilised; the crew were free to go ashore but not
to leave the town. They were very fed up with their conditions

and way of life. We met them often when ashore and as some spoke good English there was lots of conversation but they were not allowed to board our vessel.

Most foreign seamen can speak English, or can at least make themselves understood. Officers from most countries have to pass an examination in English when sitting for their Certificates of Competency. The British seafarers were different. They never had to bother as English was the international language of the sea. We had the biggest Merchant Navy in the world and had ships sailing to every corner of the globe. Wherever you went, shipping business and bar business was conducted in English. The British seaman always learned a few words in the language of the host country, just basic phrases to express the needs of the time.

One night when ashore I was talking to an engineer from the Danish ship. He asked me if he and some others could come on board the night before we sailed and come with us to England in order that they might help in some way to liberate their country which had been occupied by the Germans in April 1940. I talked with some of the other officers on board and it was agreed that we would help them. The first thing was to prepare a hiding place. I thought the after peak would be ideal. We would be fully laden and the tank would be empty. The tank lid was in the steering flat so we went back on board and unscrewed all the bolts and removed the lid to ventilate the tank. Just before dawn the engineer and five others came on board and went into the after peak. Before sailing the lid was carefully placed on the studs with wedges placed underneath and the bolts loosely turned to allow some passage of air. The local pilot arrived on board together with the Harbour Master, the Police

Chief and other harbour authorities. They must have asked the Captain if there were any of the Danish crew on board, as the three officers were sent for, Mate, 2nd Mate (myself) and 3rd Mate, and told to search the ship. I elected to search the after deck. The Captain and the Mate knew nothing of our illicit operation. After a while I reported back to the Captain in his cabin that none but our own crew were on board, but later I was asked to search again. This time I took the 3rd Mate with me, who was in the know. We reported back as before – no unauthorised persons on board. We were then allowed to sail.

Among the crew and DEMS gunners we had three musicians, or rather players of instruments. As soon as we were clear of the quay they stood on the after gun platform and started some jazz tune. There were lots of people on the quay waving to us and wishing us luck. Before reaching open water we passed a small bay where there were people waving to us from a white house which was flying the Union Flag. As soon as the pilot disembarked we brought the stowaways out and gave them a meal. They soon found jobs for themselves in the different departments; one was a 3rd Engineer.

Not at the time but many years later I wondered why we should make such a long voyage to Montevideo with coal. The voyage did, of course, earn precious currency and we were not too far from Vitoria where we loaded our vital cargo of ore.

We were now homeward bound but not sailing directly to the UK. We headed north up the Brazilian coast. Next stop would be St. Lucia for bunkers – sailing independently – then to Norfolk, Virginia and to Halifax, Nova Scotia to the convoy assembly anchorages at Bedford Basin.

We were only in St. Lucia for about six hours, just long

enough to replenish our coal bunkers and to top-up our fresh water tanks. As I was not actively involved in loading the coal and as the Chief Officer had no objections, I went, together with the 3rd Mate, for a stroll ashore. The town of Port Castries on the island was not very big in those days and we were soon in the main part of town. We did manage to stop at a convenient bar for refreshments. On the way back we passed a school and could hear children singing. The sound of children's voices struck a chord after the months away from home. Assisted by the effects of our refreshments we decided to enter the school and see as well as hear. We were dressed in tropical gear – white shirts with epaulettes and uniform caps. As we neared the classroom we were spotted by the teacher who immediately brought to a halt the song being rendered. When we were ushered into the classroom she brought the children to attention and then struck up the National Anthem. To hear them singing 'God save our King' with their sweet little voices so many thousands of miles away from Britain made two very sheepish Merchant Navy officers very humble and I know what it means to have a lump in the throat.

Our Danish guests on board remained at their duties. There was no attempt to desert their new abode or the friends they had already made.

After St. Lucia it was then up to Norfolk, Virginia for further stores and routing. Just a few hours there and then we were hugging the coast up to Halifax. Bedford Basin, Halifax was the main assembly harbour for eastern-bound convoys. The entrance had a naval boom with anti-submarine nets to prevent any enemy infiltration. It had served this same purpose during the Great War of 1914–18. On occasions you could wait for days until a sufficient number of ships could be gathered together to form a large enough convoy to warrant the naval escort appointed.

I thought, one night, when keeping anchor watch, seeing the numerous other vessels around me and watching others arriving and entering the Basin through the boom, of the gigantic explosion which occurred during the 1914–18 War when two vessels collided, one being full of munitions which caused a massive explosion with devastating results. There was at that time one of my present Company's ships lying at anchor. She was not damaged but stories were told years after that the Master was just arriving back on board after being ashore at the agents and at the time of the explosion was going up the accommodation ladder holding his briefcase which contained quite a lot of money. It was, unfortunately, blown out of his grasp by the terrific blast of the explosion. The money had to be claimed for. Perhaps the person who started this rumour was not too fond of the Captain!

After a few days we were on our way across the Atlantic again – back in the firing line, you might say. The U-Boats were extending their operations further and further west. There was added protection now by longer range coastal command aircraft like the Catalina operations from Iceland, and US surface craft.

The month of October was not a particularly bad month for casualties in the Atlantic or in this eastbound convoy. The evasive actions and courses, plus routing, could have contributed to this. Evasive routing was the way the Admiralty described it.

Before leaving we knew our destination. On this occasion it was to be Middlesbrough, with first a stop at Loch Ewe where the convoy would split into west and east coast sections. It was then through the Pentland Firth to the next assembly anchorage in the Firth of Forth off Methil. And then down to the Tees in convoy.

It was dark when we tied up at our allocated berth in Middlesbrough which was on the port side of the river near the town and up river from the old transporter bridge. No sooner had we completed mooring than there was the sound of marching feet and orders being shouted. I looked over the side and saw about a dozen soldiers lined up near the gangway with rifles at the ready. They looked like the Home Guard. They had come to take away our Danish stowaways who had, of course, been reported at every stop. Our 'guests' had been on board for forty-four days and firm friendships had been made with those with whom they had worked. They had also been a great asset on board, being very good seamen, turning their hand to anything. It seemed to me an ignoble end to their efforts to get back to the UK and help in whichever way they could to free their homeland. They were put into a truck and driven off. We heard later that they were sent immediately to London by train to be interrogated. It was a sad sight watching them being taken away in this fashion. They could have stayed in Vitoria and enjoyed a quiet peaceful life until the war ended or at least until Brazil threw her lot in with the Allies. This didn't happen until August 1942 and it was now November 1941. We heard no more but I often wondered what became of them. I hoped that they would eventually get safely back to their homes and people.

* * *

After discharging our cargo at Middlesbrough, our orders were to proceed to Leith. We wondered what next? What could we

*The author as 2nd Officer of
SS* Lowther Castle.

load there and for where? We were certainly not going back across the Atlantic light ship to bring another cargo of food or war material and ammunition back to the UK. After a couple of days of speculation we learned our fate. We were to take supplies to our then ally, Russia. There were lots of preparations to be made: the lower hods had to be prepared for the carriage of tanks and the DB tanks and bilges had to be protected. They were covered in the customary manner by soft wood timber laid in lengths of 7″ wide by 2½–3″ thick which, of course, was called by seafaring folk the 'ceiling'. This was the correct term for the tank top protection in all seamanship manuals. This, however, would be no protection against the tearing up of the wood by the tractors of the tanks as they were manoeuvred into position and secured. To combat this a layer of shingle about six inches deep was laid over the 'ceiling'. It was not only the holds which had to be prepared but also those who manned the vessel.

It was now December and to combat the severe conditions soon to be encountered meant providing extra heating in the accommodation. This was done by fitting a small solid fuel stove in each officer's cabin with a smoke outlet or chimney sticking out through the deck above. We used to joke about how many funnels the ship had. We also had to be supplied with appropriate gear or wearing apparel to keep watch on the bridge. Clothing was supplied by the Ministry to protect us in the arctic weather. This consisted of – starting from the inside – two pairs of heavy woollen ribbed Long Johns, then a flannel shirt and on top of this, a rolled neck jersey. Then a sheepskin lined leather jerkin and on top of all this, a canvas dufflecoat with a hood and lined with a sort of blanket material. Heavy lined mitts covered the hands, and feet were protected by two pairs of woollen stockings reaching to the knee. The last thing on was a pair of seaboots which had to be two sizes too large to be able to be pulled on.

The rooms were warm because of the coal stove but it took some time to clothe yourself ready to venture on deck. When you did you staggered around like the astronauts landing on the moon. On one occasion when on watch in the early afternoon and when approaching the Kola Inlet I decided to take a bearing of a headland. To do this I went up to the 'Monkey Island' where the standard compass was placed. This was the ship's main compass and it was completely unprotected from the weather. It was necessary to remove the brass binnacle top covering the compass. I tried to do this but with the heavy mitts on found it quite impossible. Foolishly, I removed the mitts and grasped the two brass handles of the binnacle top. It was like receiving an electric shock. This shock made me let go immediately and this saved me from doing more serious damage to my hands. As it was I received nasty burns which took weeks to heal. With all this heavy gear on, I thought, how would I ever get into a lifeboat if the occasion arose? I am sure I would never have survived in the water. Sailing to Russia in December with limited hours of daylight had its advantages despite the arctic weather. Norway and Finland were occupied by the Germans and their bombers and torpedo bombers were constantly in action from coastal air fields. But only in daylight fortunately and there wasn't much of this. There was also a large German naval force lying in the Norwegian fjords ready to emerge and attack any convoy which could be located.

To escape from a torpedoed vessel and manage to get into a lifeboat was a hazard in itself. All the heavy clothing made movement very difficult. There was also the danger of frost-bite if in a boat or raft for any length of time in the severe arctic weather conditions.

When the ship had been satisfactorily prepared for this on-coming arctic voyage and we had all been fitted out with the appropriate clothing we moved across the Firth of Forth to the anchorage at Methil. On 10 December 1941 we sailed for Murmansk via Reykjavik, Iceland.

We encountered strong south-westerly and north-westerly gales on passage and, as well as some superficial damage, suf-fered the loss of our lifeboats. It was considered unwise to allow us to continue the voyage without our main means of survival if torpedoed, so we were ordered to proceed to a fjord a few miles from Reykjavik harbour, anchor there and await develop-ments. We were almost completely landlocked by snow covered mountains. The waters were calm and everything seemed so peaceful. It was here that we spent Christmas. The peace and quiet were most welcome after our last battle with the elements when we only averaged 6 knots for the whole voyage. However, after a while I had the feeling that we had been forgotten. We were supposed to be waiting for replacement lifeboats but these never came. After being fitted with some temporary livesaving equipment we eventually sailed on 8 February, but back to the UK and this time to Loch Ewe. The voyage was reasonably quiet and uneventful except that we had many alterations of course which we learned later were to avoid U-Boats lying ahead and waiting for us.

Our stay in Loch Ewe was brief, just one day, and we were then ready and fully equipped to proceed on our next attempt to deliver our much needed cargo to the Russians. The main convoy ready to sail for Murmansk was forming up in Kirkwall in the Orkney Islands. After the Convoy Conference and other formalities we were soon on our way and this time direct to Murmansk without a stop at Reykjavik. We kept well off the Norwegian coast to avoid, if possible, the torpedo bombers operating from there. On 20 February our noon position was 73°00′N 15°30′E and at one stage we were six hundred miles to the west of the Norwegian coast. I had not sailed in latitudes as high as this before and not many mariners engaged in commercial trade would have done so.

This second attempt to reach Murmansk took ten days and we had steamed 1,774 miles. We were anchored in the Roads for a couple of days before moving to a discharge berth.

Arriving in Russia was something different. I had been at sea for quite a long time. In my previous book, *Seafaring in the Thirties*, I recalled that at the age of twenty-two I had circumnavigated the globe ten times. That meant visiting many ports, some exciting, some beautiful, some you would not wish to see again. Entering the Kola Inlet was somehow eerie. The whole of the landscape was covered in a heavy blanket of snow and there was ice to push through. It was quiet and still and very cold. We had spent a hazardous ten days before arriving with our valuable and much needed supply of tanks, vehicles and ammunition and there was a sense of relief that we had arrived safely. We had survived what was to be later in the summer months, with its endless daylight, an extremely dangerous voyage. However, the peace and quiet of being tied up safely in harbour away from marauding submarines and enemy surface vessels was not to last for we had now to suffer attack from bomber aircraft which I presumed came from occupied Poland and Finland.

When crossing the Atlantic, no matter what disasters befell, no matter how many ships were lost, no matter how hard the weather, if you survived the crossing you were now safe. No restrictions, no air-raids, no blackout, no doubling of watches, no tired eyes trying to distinguish black from black on a dark night in convoy, no shortages ashore. A time for rest and relaxing. Certainly not here in Murmansk, which in 1942 was subjected to some of the severest air attacks on any town up to that time.

* * *

We spent four weeks in Murmansk, not all of it alongside the wharfs. I am not sure of the number of vessels in this particular convoy but of those of us who survived the voyage, there was not enough quay space to discharge all of the vessels at one time. We had to wait our turn and then, after completing discharge, lay off at anchor to await the assembly of the return convoy to the UK. My first impression of the Russians when berthing alongside and commencing to discharge was their total dedication to the war effort. No pubs, no dance halls, no time off, just work for at least twelve hours a day with just as many women doing the labouring as the men, many more in the unskilled work. We had taken with us, I think, half a dozen army personnel who were to instruct the Russians in the handling of the tanks we had landed. I was amazed to see their own drivers take them away with hardly any instruction whatsoever.

I wondered what their impressions of us were. I do not think many of the inhabitants of Murmansk had ever seen or met a British or American person. There was no possibility that they could have travelled very far from their own locality. It was not just the cost of travel but also, in the Russia of this day, there was no freedom of travel and visas for leaving the country were strictly forbidden. There were very few of even the most world travelled seamen, myself included, who had ever been to these parts. Before leaving Leith it was decided among some of the officers that we would not shave but would grow beards and look as we imagined a Russian would look when we arrived in Murmansk. My effort was not very successful for I had a bald patch on each side of my chin below the lips. It didn't matter much for on arrival we found that we were the only ones with beards. Ivan the Terrible characters were nowhere to be seen.

Our relations with the local inhabitants were very cordial, but not overwhelmingly friendly. They, no doubt, were pleased with our efforts to assist them in the continued resolve to defeat the Nazi menace. Overall, I sensed a feeling that they were not free to say or do as they wished.

There was, as might be expected in these circumstances, a small black market. (The black market was very illegal and warranted severe punishment.) There was no conversation, for they could speak as much English as we could speak Russian, practically nil. We had nothing to barter with except cigarettes. If ashore you could be stopped or walked alongside by a person offering you cash for cigarettes. Those who had succumbed to the temptation of making a quick buck later found that the Russian currency was worthless outside the USSR. It could be used to purchase a cheap beer and vodka in the one place ashore where we could avail ourselves of some seamanlike activity. I seem to recall that the only place where there was this sort of shore life was in the 'Atlantic Hotel'. I may have the name wrong but it was the only refuge for a weary mariner. We just sat at a table in a rather large room and were served by a waitress with drinks which were strictly rationed: so many per person and no more. If you had been successfully or otherwise accosted on the street then your pocket would be bulging with useless roubles.

When I first stepped ashore in Murmansk it was the first time I had been on land or off the ship since 7 December. It was now 25 February, so I had been cooped up for eighty days.

A remarkable incident happened one evening when sitting in the 'Atlantic' or was it 'Arctic'? A Polish major staying in the hotel spoke to me. Perhaps I looked the sympathetic type for he looked so down and miserable. He invited me to his room for a drink and there related a most remarkable and sinister account of how he came to be there.

Despite the carve up of Poland by the pact between Stalin and Hitler, Poland was by now completely occupied by the Nazis. The Russians were now our allies, both of us fighting the more evil tyrant. It was, of course, the invasion of Poland which caused Britain and then France to declare war on Germany.

He told me how he had been abducted in the middle of the night by Russian agents, leaving behind his wife and family, and taken to North Russia so that he could organise a contingent of Polish refugees and form a fighting force within the USSR army to fight against the Germans. He had, of course, no option. History now reveals that thousands of Polish army officers were murdered and buried in shallow graves by the Russian forces. This carnage is now admitted by the present régime. He was pleased that we had at last come to the aid of his nation but was shocked and bitter about his treatment, just as I was. He didn't invite the Germans or the Russians into his country. I thought, here am I risking my life bringing war supplies to a nation who could behave in this manner; but they were now our allies with just one aim – to defeat the Nazis. We chatted for some time, unknown, I would think, to the others in the hotel. In the part of the hotel where we were allowed to have a drink we were limited to the amount we could buy. I think at this time it was only a couple of vodkas per person. I was pleased to listen to this officer's story and enjoyed his company. I also enjoyed his hospitality for he had a bottle of vodka which I would describe as 'the real stuff'.

It had been snowing for some time and it was very thick on the ground. The pavements were kept clear but not in the manner I had seen at home. The snow was piled up at the edge of the pavement or walkway in a shape like a garden fence about five feet high. There were gaps to allow entry to and from the pavement inside. It seemed to me a good idea for it was certainly not going to melt and become slush in this north Russian temperature in mid-winter. In any case, there would not be the labour available to remove it for as I have remarked before there was certainly full commitment to the war effort with most of the workforce discharging the vessels and loading the rail trucks being female. Not that you could tell the difference for everyone was dressed alike. One noticeable difference in their footwear was that whereas we had been issued with large rubber seaboots to fit over double heavy socks, their footwear of the same size appeared to be made of some sort of felt material. They could walk along the icy roads without falling over. We had to walk very gingerly and I spent a lot of time getting up again. Rubber and ice were not compatible.

After saying goodnight and goodbye to the Major, who was

moving on the next day, I started to wend my way back on board. It's amazing the effect arctic cold air can have on you when stepping outside from a warm hotel lobby. I should have walked straight towards the gap in the snow wall or fence ahead, but instead I veered a little to starboard and put my face into the snow. I was fortunate that someone else had left at the same time or I would have had a badly frost-bitten face. The vodka must certainly have been 'the real stuff'.

I hoped that the Russian counter-offensive was helped by the Allies supplying them with arms and equipment in the most hazardous conditions and seaways. It was well under way by this time and we were invited to see a film taken by a Russian army official photographer of their troops recapturing a small town or village which had been occupied by the German army. This was real action which was most brutal. When the tanks moved into the main square, the sight that met them must have made them furious and their reactions understandable. Strung between light standards were wires and from them the bodies of dozens of local inhabitants hanging by the neck. The Germans had obviously left them as they retreated. Russian infantrymen were sitting on the tanks, as many as could possibly be carried. They jumped off immediately and ran towards the buildings in the square. Not all of the German troops had managed to escape and some were found hiding in cellars. Perhaps they thought the retreat would be more hazardous and they could now surrender and stay alive. This was not to be, for we saw German troops coming out of buildings and cellars with gratings on the pavement, with their hands held high in token of surrender. Prisoners were not in the minds of the liberating Russian soldiers and we saw the immediate killing of all who crawled out of their rat holes either by shooting or by bayonet. The Russians had suffered terribly and the sight of those bodies swinging by the neck must have incensed them.

To me, a remarkable scene during this film was of people greeting the troops by making the sign of the cross and by some kneeling as they did so in this most significant display of Christian faith. Russia at this time was an atheist state. Stalin had banned all religion. Churches had been ransacked or closed and it was an offence to practise your spiritual beliefs and commitments. So to see these people manifesting their beliefs in front of cameras that were only there to record the liberation of this community and counter-offensive of the Red Army, was to me quite amazing. The Kremlin's decree had been to abolish religion and, in some instances, to make it an offence to be seen or caught practising it. It could be said that those seen in this stark account were of the older generation. That is true because, as I said of my immediate impression when arriving in Murmansk, the war effort was total and the younger folk, male and female, would be fully engaged in waging war against the Nazi invaders. Still, these older people were once young people and had kept their faith which would surely be passed on. Today this is clearly so.

This behaviour seemed even more remarkable when I thought about it afterwards because we were then shown another film which was nothing else but an anti-religious film which did all it could to ridicule and lampoon the Christian faith. I must admit it was at times very funny. But the underlying message, or rather the overriding one, was that religion was bogus bunkum or whatever you would like to call it. The story was based on the adventures of two supposedly escaped convicts. They were first seen in a church during mass, making themselves inconspicuous among the parishioners. There were also close ups of them making rude gestures. When the service was over the priest, who was shown as a huge, fat, well-fed person, was seated at the entrance to the church and beside him was a huge tub. This apparently was for the faithful to put money into and they were expected to fill it. If they did not offer enough they were abused and shouted at by the priest until they gave more and I suppose all that they had. When our two 'heroes' departed they had nothing to give and in order to avoid being attacked and maybe arrested, they managed to escape and fled from the area. Next we saw the priest with his fellow clergy counting what was obviously meant to be the day's takings. They didn't bother to count each separate note but just put a hand into the tub and brought out a fistful of rouble notes saying, 'That must be a hundred or maybe two hundred,' and filled sacks while at the same time taking large swallows of vodka.

Meanwhile, the stars of the show had travelled miles away and were now seen sheltering in a convent where they had asked for sanctuary. There were no actual scenes of sexual contact between the nuns and the reprobates but they were shown nipping in and out of various rooms which was meant to give you the impression that this was so. They had by now changed their clothing and were draped in long white gowns. The convent was on a hill and the word was passed to the many villages in the valleys below that a Messiah or prophet would appear on a certain day at a certain hour. Before the event we saw hundreds and hundreds of villagers trekking over the plains and up the hill to the gates of the convent. When enough people had gathered before the gates, the Messiah, in his white robes, appeared before them. He uttered some well chosen prayers which made some of the crowd fall to their knees. In the crowd of apparently devout people was the other partner who must have slipped out of the back door. He was dressed in peasant gear and had acquired from somewhere a pair of crutches; he was now a very sad cripple hoping for a miracle cure at the hands of the bogus Messiah. After a while No. 1 spotted No. 2 who was very prominent in the crowd and beckoned him to come forward towards him. Hands were placed on his head, eyes lifted upwards and hey-presto the cripple threw his crutches high into the air and started to perform an acrobatic act which would have done justice to the famous Moscow Circus. Handsprings, back somersaults, it was all there. This caused the crowd to surge forward to acclaim the so-called Messiah. In the confusion that followed our two made their get-away.

This film was quite simply to show to the people of the western world, whom they have now made contact with, just how ridiculous religion is. This was in sharp contrast to what we had seen in the first film when the villagers had unashamedly demonstrated their feelings and beliefs. That film was, of course, of the actual action and could not have been edited. Although the Russian people must have been pleased to see us, if only for the reason which brought us there, we never had any real intimate contact with them. The language barrier, of course, did not help.

One morning the Captain, with his senior officers, was sitting in the saloon having a morning coffee. For some of us it was 'having a warm' after being on deck supervising the discharging operations. In practice, all ships when in port have an agent appointed by the company or owners of the vessel whose task it is to look after the welfare and needs of the Master and his vessel. They look after port formalities, customs, harbour rules and advance of cash, relay messages and orders from the owners, and handle the ship's mail. We found this different in Murmansk. The person appointed to look after the vessel's interests was a government agent employed by them to give us instructions rather than advice. This same morning whilst sipping our coffee there was a bit of banter going and jokes were being told by one or another. I had just finished telling what I thought was a funny story when in walked the agent. I remarked, 'Perhaps he can tell us one now.' There was a strong silence and he requested that the Captain took him up to his private quarters. They hadn't been up there many minutes before I was sent for. The agent wanted to know what I had meant by my remark and seemed to think he had been insulted. I was asked by the Captain to apologise which I did, saying no offence was intended. Returning to the saloon, I told the others who were quite amazed. We knew that soon we would be leaving the berth to go to an anchorage and shore leave would be cancelled.

Russian currency was worthless outside the country and as I had quite a few notes I found the largest denomination, rolled it into a tube, put the end into the solid fuel heater in the saloon and lit my cigarette with it. This caused some laughter and I was lucky that the overbearing agent did not appear again or I might have been transported to the salt mines.

This little incident did not in any way alter my first impression on arriving in Murmansk which was of their total commitment to the war effort.

The next day we moved out of the harbour to an anchorage to await the completion of discharge of other vessels and so form a homeward bound convoy. The temperature dropped lower and lower and the whole of our sanitary system became frozen. Certain elementary functions were done by half filling a bucket with snow, bringing it into the toilet and then throwing it over the side.

* * *

It was now March 1942 and I had made numerous voyages across the North Atlantic, including the famous *Jervis Bay* convoy, and a convoy where we had to take evasive action and alteration of course to avoid oil tankers which had been torpedoed in the middle of the night and were alight and spilling their blazing cargo on the waters. I had been up to now very lucky and, looking back, I cannot imagine what possessed me to embark on the following venture which could have cost me my life.

After a few days at anchor I went on deck one morning and found the vessel completely icebound. We seemed to be locked solid in the ice. There was no movement of the ship at all by either current or wind. I decided it would be a good idea to go on the ice, walk about a bit and take a photograph of my floating home to have as a souvenir. A pilot ladder was put over the side abreast of No. 2 hatch and down I went, clutching a broom handle to use as a steadying stick and to probe the thickness of the ice as I moved further away from the hull. There were not many watching me and I had not made any provision for any sort of rescue if I had slipped and could not keep my feet; there was not even anybody standing by with a heaving line to throw to me. I was quite confident and even thought of walking right around the vessel. I had gone about twenty feet in a direct line from the pilot ladder when my broom handle, which I held before me, sank into the ice and I almost fell over it. I was terrified: what a way to end after the charmed life I had had up till now. I literally crawled on my hands and knees slowly back to the safety of the pilot ladder. I had been seen; heaving lines were thrown and I was helped up the ladder. I think I was more scared crawling back to the ship than ever I was under enemy attack. At least then you thought it wouldn't happen to you, whereas in attempting my stupid walkabout I had myself created a situation wherein I could so easily have lost my life.

* * *

We had now been in Murmansk for four weeks and the time had come for us to return to the UK. For some ships this meant another daunting challenge to arrive safely, re-load and return with another cargo of supplies. Others could be required to undertake perhaps less hazardous voyages to other parts of the world to bring much needed supplies to the homeland.

As we were making ready to depart, our sister ship, the *Lancaster Castle*, arrived and passed close to us in the Kola Inlet. The Captain of the *Lancaster Castle*, J. Sloan, had newly been appointed. He was a personal friend of mine and we had sailed together on different ships for a long time. When I was a junior apprentice he was a senior apprentice; when I was a senior apprentice he was the 3rd Officer; and on the *Lancaster Castle* I was the 2nd Officer and he was the Chief Officer. We had also shared digs in Liverpool when studying for our certificates, he, of course, taking a higher grade. I had hopes that we might meet up again but this was not to be, for on 14 April 1942 his ship was bombed in the harbour. He escaped serious injury but unfortunately lost his life whilst being taken back to England on one of HM vessels. It was necessary to get him home as soon as possible in order that he might command another vessel. Qualified Masters were essential to the whole structure and manning of the Merchant Navy.

Despite the appalling losses of ships and men, I was only once on a vessel with an uncertificated navigating officer. This one exception was on the *Lancaster Castle*, one voyage when the 3rd Officer was uncertificated. He was, however, an ex-apprentice in the company and was known to both the Chief Officer and myself. There were other companies who had to engage uncertificated officers but only in the most junior rank. One concession from the Department of Trade was that the sea time spent between studying and sitting the examination of a higher grade was reduced. Two years became eighteen months, eighteen months became twelve months, but the examinations were just the same. There was no quick promotion in the Merchant Navy, no pips in the field or a higher rank given when at sea. Except, of course, for the Chief Officer who had to possess a Master Mariner's Certificate. This was necessary should he have to take command owing to the illness or death of the Captain. The time spent between the grades mentioned above had to be spent actually at sea.

We left in darkness, hoping to be well clear of the land when daylight came and so avoid being seen leaving the Kola Inlet. Every effort was made to avoid the marauding U-Boats and any surface craft searching the northern seas for such as us. The weather was not bad at first but later deteriorated and became what one would expect of these waters in March.

On the fifth day we encountered strong north-easterly gales

and were wallowing about in heavy seas. The next day we found ourselves alone, the convoy having been scattered by the weather conditions. We received instructions to make for Reykjavik in Iceland. This gave us respite from the north-easterly gales but also meant that we would have complete air-cover. It took us ten days; our average speed over this period was 7½ knots and the distance steamed 1,800 miles.

After three days and a false start due to dense fog, we were on our way bound for Loch Ewe, the convoy assembly haven on the west coast of Scotland. We had the honour to be made Commodore of this nine-vessel convoy. I have seen the report of the escort commander on our armed trawler, which reads: 'The convoy was conducted in a most efficient manner by Commodore (*Lowther Castle*), whose signalling was of a high standard'. I don't remember being that good! Most of the day-light lamp signalling must have been when I was off watch. Flag signals, yes – morse, no.

We made one large diversion after a report that U-Boats were lying in wait ahead of us. This happened often on North Atlantic voyages. The weather again was what could be expected but we arrived safely in Loch Ewe. Over two days with strong easterly gales we averaged no more than 3.5 knots; being light ship made progress very difficult. It was here that we were given our final destination. It was to be West Hartlepool on the north-east coast. It seemed ironic that having come westward through the turbulent waters of the Pentland Firth in darkness and observing a complete blackout, we now had to navigate these waters again in the opposite direction to reach our final destination. The weather was kinder to us now but there was still one more stop on the way, Methil in the Firth of Forth.

We were not there very long; the visit was just so that we could receive further routing and escort to proceed further south. It was a Sunday when we arrived and in the evening near the dock a Salvation Army Band was playing in what you could call a familiar position outside a pub. Hymns were being sung and we were now back to normal in the UK.

I had forgotten that before leaving the quay in Murmansk a number of long crates had been loaded on board. They had been well lashed and had not moved during the bad weather. It was not until they had been discharged that I learned that they were torpedoes which were found to be unsuitable for whatever USSR submarines they were intended for. I have heard stories about a British oil tanker laden with aviation spirit which could not be used in some Russian aircraft.

I had by now more than the required sea time in my present rank necessary to be accepted in the Nautical College to study for my final certificate, that of Master Mariner. This certificate was needed if I wanted promotion to 1st Mate, or eventually Master, so I felt it was something I had to do. There was a time when you could do some studying for exams when at sea, but not now with the constant tension and watches being frequently doubled.

I asked to be relieved and in a few days' time I was on my way home.

The *Lowther Castle* returned to Murmansk on her next voyage but unfortunately she was torpedoed and sunk by enemy aircraft sixty miles east-south-east of Bear Island, approximately 70°N 21°E. This was a bad period for the owners. In March the *Muncaster Castle* had been sunk. In April the *Lancaster Castle*, in May the *Lowther Castle*. The previous year the *Wray Castle*

Lowther Castle (*from a model made by the author*) *returning from Murmansk, showing all convoy signals.*

had been lost. The *Bolton Castle* was way up north in position 76°40′N 36°30′E when she was torpedoed and sunk. This was in Convoy PQ17 in which twenty-four ships were sunk out of the total of thirty-nine which set out.

Chapter 4

SS *Pollux II*

IT was now the end of April 1942 and I arrived home with the firm intention of having a break from the sea and then enroling in the Nautical College to study for my final examinations, for Master Mariner. I had been away for nine months and felt I was due for a short break, especially after my last two voyages to Murmansk. I had planned to start studying after about two weeks. Plans don't work out as originally devised and in a couple of weeks' time I was back at sea again.

One day I went to Liverpool from my home in Chester to see if any of my old friends were at the Nautical College or home on leave. I knew where I could find them. They would be in our favourite watering hole, the Villiers, the pub in Elliot Street kept by that grand lady Mrs Shepherd, known worldwide as 'Ma Shepherd' of whom I wrote in my book *Seafaring in the Thirties*. She would be able to tell me who had recently been home, what ship so and so had joined and, with real tears, those who would not be returning. There I was introduced to a Captain Naarits, an Estonian in command of the vessel *Pollux II*. He had managed to bring his vessel over to the UK from somewhere in the Baltic when war broke out. The *Pollux II* was now under the Red Ensign and registered in Glasgow. She was a small vessel now trading around the coast carrying vital equipment from the smaller ports to the larger ones and supplying the small ports with coal and grain. Captain Naarits was looking for a 1st Mate and offered me the position. I had been sailing as 2nd Mate with a foreign 1st Mate's Certificate so was eligible to sail as 1st Mate in the coastal or short sea trade. He invited me to go on board with him and see his vessel. I had an idea that he was part owner. We went by taxi to the dock where his vessel was lying undergoing some minor repairs. I was not very impressed; she was certainly not 'shipshape and Bristol fashion', and the 1st Mate's cabin, although quite roomy, looked very dowdy. Of course, I had to consider that if I accepted his offer it would amount to promotion. Because of the size of the vessel only two mates were required to comply with Board of Trade Regulations and she was now a British registered vessel.

I was introduced to the Chief and 2nd Engineers who were both Estonian and then, to my surprise, found that the catering staff, chief steward, steward and cook were all female. They were also Estonians. I had heard of Baltic owned ships having female personnel in the catering department but had never envisaged it happening on British registered vessels. I was reluctant to accept the position but then thought that as the 1st Mate and second in command, I would be able to bring the ship up to scratch, and make her more like the vessels I had been used to sailing on. I would also earn more money, which would be needed when I enrolled at the Nautical College, for I would have to pay a fee, buy more textbooks and pay for lodgings in Liverpool.

It seemed that Captain Naarits was impressed by what I told him I could do. I was also most impressed with him. Here was a man who must have had a hazardous time bringing his vessel to Britain and who was prepared to serve the right cause. It was this that finally made me accept his offer and I decided to join the *Pollux II* as 1st Mate. I boarded the vessel a few days later in Garston, up river from Liverpool, where she was loading a full cargo of coal for Dartmouth to be discharged in Kingswear.

On entering my cabin I was struck by the change. I had a new carpet, new mattress and bed clothes, and new bright curtains for both the bunk and the two portholes. Captain Naarits certainly made me welcome on board. We sailed in convoy around the coast and as I was familiar with routing instructions etc., I had few problems. She was not a very powerful vessel and we frequently fell behind in convoy. We were often a straggler and had a job to get back in the fold.

Meal times were a little strange to me. If I was keeping an evening watch, from 4 p.m., I would be called at 3.30 and before going on the bridge would go to the saloon or messroom and on the table would be plates of sliced sausages, biscuits, tomatoes, bread and coffee, a sort of snack before ascending the bridge ladder. It was not meant to be a meal but sort of a 'put you on'. Later, I was relieved to have a proper evening meal. I got to like this way of feeding, but couldn't help wondering where the food came from!

There were things that every good Chief Officer does daily in larger vessels and usually in port in two watch vessels. That is to go round the ship, go to all parts and departments, and check if things are correct. I was now in that role so on the first day in Kingswear I decided to practise what I had been taught. Having been for'd and inspected the seamen's quarters (which were still under the fo'c'slehead, which gave some idea of the age of the vessel) and seen that the bow moorings were secure,

I was now on my way aft with the galley the next on my mental list. I was about to step over the threshold, when I was confronted by a plumpish middle-aged lady blocking my path. It was the Estonian cook who conveyed to me in a few barely understandable English words, accompanied by forceful gesticulations, that this was her galley, her domain and no one could enter unless she said so. I got the message loud and clear and from what I could see from the doorway the place was absolutely spotless. I must add that after being on board a few weeks 'Madam Cook' and I became quite good friends and I was even allowed in.

Subsequent voyages were similar to the first one and were confined to the west coast and south coast of England and Wales. This was preferable to trading on the east coast where enemy air attacks were frequent and expected. We did have our scares, of course, but they were mostly ineffective air attacks from one or two enemy planes.

On one other voyage to Kingswear with a cargo of coal we heard that the King was arriving to present medals to the brave men who had manned the MTBs, which had attacked a French Channel port successfully, though with some losses. There had been many minor sorties of this nature but this one had greater significance and the town of Dartmouth was very proud of its MTB Flotilla. The rail line to Dartmouth ended at Kingswear on the opposite side of the River Dart. Our discharging berth was quite near to the station so I went along to witness the arrival of His Majesty, King George VI. I was most surprised when he stepped off the train near to where I was standing. He was in full naval uniform and as he came abreast of where I stood I saw what I thought was a much younger man. I was very close to him and got the impression that he had been carefully made up before leaving the train. There must have been a make-up artist travelling with him to prepare him to meet the public. He was most revered by the nation for his stance in refusing to leave Buckingham Palace and the capital during the fiercest of the enemy blitz. Star treatment was certainly in order.

My time on the *Pollux II* came to an end in August 1942. She was quite an old vessel and needed extensive repairs in order to keep her functioning as a valuable cog in the chain of smaller coastal vessels carrying much needed cargoes of materials to the smaller ports. It was decided by the Ministry that she should be dry-docked and given a complete overhaul. A dry dock and ship repair firm in Port Talbot, South Wales, was appointed to carry out all that was necessary. I doubt if the venue had anything to do with tendering but was just because the dry dock was available and convenient considering our trading pattern on the west coast. With the knowledge that the *Pollux II* was going into dry dock and the articles of agreement between Master and crew would be terminated, I decided that this time after paying and signing off I would do what I had originally planned to do. That was to go home, have a short break, then enrol in the Nautical College in Liverpool and seriously get down to studying so as to sit the examinations for my final certificate, that of Master Mariner.

I had enjoyed my time on the *Pollux II*. It certainly was not wasted for I was still filling a vital role in keeping the Merchant Navy at sea. I also gained valuable experience in the handling of coastal craft which was to serve me in good stead later in my career. A couple of times when in port in the Manchester Ship Canal I had been able to slip home for a night.

Once again my plans were thwarted by the persuasive Captain Naarits. He had to go to London and asked me if I would standby the vessel as his representative during the dry-docking and see that all repairs were carried out as agreed in the specification. There would be no facilities for anyone to live on board so he arranged for me and the Chief Engineer to have private lodgings ashore with full board and expenses and adequate remuneration.

* * *

When the repairs were completed, and after enjoying a short break, I enrolled in the Nautical College in Liverpool. I was determined to really get down to it. I kept in touch with Captain Naarits for a while and on one occasion he wrote advising me on how to master a certain problem in one of the subjects I was studying. It was the Deviascope and others had found it hard to assimilate at first but after a while all became clear.

I was fortunate to pass in all subjects and was now a Certificated Master. I had spent the final few weeks in lodgings in Liverpool so as to really concentrate on the work in hand with no distractions. I returned home on the Saturday afternoon after spending some time with colleagues in our favourite watering hole, celebrating our success.

My father asked why I was home; had I given up studying? 'No Sir,' said I, 'We had the results yesterday and I have passed.' He then said, 'Good. We had better have a drink then.' We were always good friends but there was never any fuss. There was never any fuss either when I first went away at sixteen. We were a seafaring family – grandfather, father, uncles, cousins and brothers – and these things were expected. I remember that

CERTIFICATE OF COMPETENCY

AS

MASTER

OF A FOREIGN-GOING STEAMSHIP

No. *49218.*

To *Ronald Francis McBrearty.*

WHEREAS you have been found duly qualified to fulfil the duties of Master of a Foreign-going Steamship in the Merchant Service, the Minister of War Transport, in pursuance of the Merchant Shipping Acts, the Minister of Shipping (Transfer of Functions) Order, 1939, and the Ministers of the Crown (Minister of War Transport) Order, 1941, hereby grants you this Certificate of Competency.

SIGNED BY AUTHORITY OF THE MINISTER OF WAR TRANSPORT and dated this ....*22nd*........... day of ....*October,*........... 19*42.*

Countersigned *(Sgd.) G.J. Knight.*
Assistant Registrar General

Deputy Director General,
Ministry of War Transport. *C.R.*

REGISTERED AT THE OFFICE OF THE REGISTRAR GENERAL OF SHIPPING AND SEAMEN.

Master's Certificate.

MERCHANT NAVY A/A GUNNERY COURSE.

CERTIFICATE OF PROFICIENCY

3 - NOV 1942

D.E.M.S. TRAINING CENTRE,

LIVERPOOL

Date Stamp of Training Centre.

Pool.

Name ...... Mc BREARTY.

Rank or Rating.......... Mate.

B. of T. or D.B. No.

has completed the Merchant Navy A/A Gunnery
Course and is qualified in the firing and cleaning
and oiling of *...... Hotchkiss, Lewis & Marlin.

Rank ....

D.E.M.S.
Training Centre.

COMMANDER,
OFFICER-IN-CHARGE,
D.E.M.S. TRAINING CENTRE,
LIVERPOOL. **10863**

* Insert types of guns and/or A/A devices.

(22/5/42) (1961) Wt. 30644/P6516 30M 10/42 S.E.R. Ltd. Gp. 671 [OVER

2 days course.

A/A Gunnery Course.

when I obtained my first Officer's Certificate, that of 2nd Mate in 1936, some other successful candidates were given a present by their parents of a sextant to mark their achievement of 'getting on the Bridge'. I bought myself a second-hand one and carried it with me throughout the war. All navigating officers had to have their own sextant which they took from ship to ship.

Before reporting for sea service I attended a course called 'Merchant Navy A/A Gunnery'. It took place in one of the numerous warehouses or dock sheds as they were called, which lined the quaysides of the huge Merseyside dock complex. Alas, very few of them exist today. The instructors were Royal Navy petty officers and they taught us how to strip clean and load such equipment as Hotchkiss Lewis and Marlin guns. After this came the firing practice. This had to be seen to be believed.

The warehouses were large with a vast open space between ceiling and floor. Their function was to store accumulating cargo in readiness for loading onto a vessel for export. They were also used to store import cargo to await collection by the various consignees. Steel wires were attached to positions under the roof of one of the empty sheds and then led directly down at different angles and were securely anchored in the stone base floor to keep the wire rigid. Fitted to the wires were models of German planes. To simulate an air attack, the PO Instructor would release a plane which would come hurtling down the wire at great speed. The pupil stood behind a replica machine gun which fired small ball bearings. The object was to hit the model plane and the exercise was to teach you when and when not to fire and to keep the plane in your sights. You would follow the path taken by the ball bearings as if it was tracer ammunition. To fire too late would be a waste of ammunition. It seemed at first a

'Heath Robinson' operation, but it certainly made sense when you followed the arc taken by the ball bearings. I had practised with these types of A/A guns on both the *Lancaster Castle* and the *Lowther Castle*, which had them mounted on the bridge wings. It was only practice, just firing into the air, but after this course I felt confident enough to handle the weapon more efficiently if I had to.

About this time one of my three brothers had joined a vessel called the *Ardeola* as 2nd Mate. She was owned by a famous Liverpool Company, Yeoward Brothers. I think there were five vessels in the fleet and their trade was to and from the Canary Islands. General cargo was carried outwards and bananas and other fruits on the home run. They also carried passengers and were, in fact, very well known small passenger vessels with excellent facilities. They had a distinctive shape and look. I visited my brother on board in Garston and could see that alterations to the profile of the vessel had taken place. Guns were removed and she was painted in normal ship colours, but not that of the Yeoward Line. In fact an attempt had been made to make her look like some other neutral vessel. As I remember, the Yeoward Fleet had three or four masts but now there remained only two. The voyage was to be to Malta with supplies mostly medical. Once in the Mediterranean she would be dispatched from the convoy and then, with lights on and no blackout and I believe flying a neutral flag or maybe a French or Italian one, steam along the African coast and then make a determined run towards Malta. Unfortunately, the plan failed, for off Bizerta she was circled by enemy planes, recognised as not being as represented. She was then ordered into Bizerta and made captive. The crew were all made prisoners and were kept in a camp well inside the country. The battle of El Alamein began on 23 October 1942 but it was not until 7 May 1943 that Bizerta was captured.

When it was evident that the Allied advance was unstoppable and that they would soon be overwhelmed, the prisoners of the *Ardeola* and, I believe, of another vessel, a Cunarder, were released and left to find their own way on foot towards the advancing armies near the coast.

Chapter 5

SS *Fort Maurepas*

WITH my new certificate I reported to my own Company, the shipowners in whose ships I had sailed for most of my time during the last ten years, as apprentice, 3rd Mate and 2nd Mate. I was looking forward to sailing with shipmates whom I had known before and who had survived many Atlantic convoy experiences. Unfortunately they were unable to offer me a position as they had suffered heavy losses with half the fleet having been sunk, four of them in Arctic waters. Most of them I had sailed on earlier. Officers who had survived the sinking of their vessels were, of course, offered any vacancy in what remained of the fleet.

Long before the war there were plans being devised to ensure that in the event of a war the Merchant Navy could be effectively manned. At first all Merchant Navy personnel were classed as being in a reserved occupation and could not, therefore, be called up for other duties. It was essential that as the war progressed and Merchant Navy casualties were mounting that a body should be formed to train and replace those who had been lost. It was the British Shipping Federation which took on this role and formed and administered the Merchant Navy Reserve Pool in April 1941.

A typical Fort ship. (Imperial War Museum)

All Merchant Navy personnel before and after the war carried with them a hard-back book with a number registered with the Ministry of Shipping. It contained a complete record of the holder: age, size, weight, height, colour of eyes, everything including a record of every ship served on with a report as to ability and character. The Merchant Navy Reserve Pool had all this information on file and was able to supply officers and ratings as requested by the numerous shipping companies.

So it was to the Officers' Pool that I reported in Liverpool and they sent me to join a vessel called the *Fort Maurepas* at the time discharging her cargo in Manchester. She was a vessel similar in size and hull shape to the Liberty ships. The accommodation layout was different and unlike the Liberty she relied on coal for her boiler fuel. A number of these vessels were built in Canada and the *Fort Maurepas*, built in Vancouver, had just completed her maiden voyage.

The accommodation on the *Fort Maurepas* was the best I had lived in during my whole career. My cabin was much bigger and the officers' saloon, usually a place to have meals in with a long table running athwartship, had a settee on the forward side and swivel bucket seats opposite with the Captain at the head of the table. There was also a part of the saloon partitioned off to form a small lounge where you could sit and talk in comfort. I was very pleased with my posting for, after all, hadn't I progressed another step up the ladder, and the vessel was brand new!

After some time discharging and then loading a full cargo of supplies for some theatre of war or outpost of the Empire which we were not aware of at the time, we eventually cast off our moorings and with the aid of two tugs, made our way down the Manchester Ship Canal to Eastham. It was a slow transit with four sets of locks to negotiate before arriving at Eastham, which held the final locks of this internal waterway. Navigation of the canal was only permitted in daylight hours and after mooring at a lay-by berth inside the locks we awaited the next daylight high water. It was then that we were spilled out of the Manchester Ship Canal and into the River Mersey with outlet to the open sea. We were not quite under way yet for we had to anchor for a while awaiting other vessels leaving Liverpool and Birkenhead to proceed to the Mersey Estuary and then join up with us and form an outward bound westward convoy.

At last we were on our way and knew our destination. It was now New Year's Eve 1942 and we were bound for Alexandria. In the present circumstances the only way we could hope to arrive there would be by sailing round the Cape of Good Hope then up the east coast of Africa, through the Red Sea and the Suez Canal and into the Mediterranean. It would be a long haul. Before the war and for many years afterwards the Manchester Ship Canal was a very busy waterway with hundreds of vessels coming from and leaving for ports all over the world. It is now sadly in decline and the port of Manchester no longer exists. Considering the importance of the canal economy and its vital role during the war, I was puzzled as to why the enemy did not mount a concerted attack on the Eastham locks to put them permanently out of action. Liverpool, across the water, was bombed heavily yet the locks remained workable. Had the attacks been successful the whole of the canal as far up as Lachford would have run into the Mersey and become tidal with the water rushing in and out causing severe damage to the banks and any craft moored in that section. Ships above Lachford would have been trapped.

After leaving the Mersey Estuary near the Bar Light Vessel, the convoy sailed up the Irish Sea and, giving the north of Ireland a wide berth, headed out into the North Atlantic.

* * *

I do not have a record of daily positions on this passage to Cape Town. As the Chief Officer or 1st Mate, I was not involved so much in the navigation of the vessel and did not always take sights in the forenoon and at midday with the Captain and the other deck officers. I did not therefore keep a Sight Book with records of daily positions, speed, distance run, weather etc. That was the role of the 2nd Mate. The Chart Room was his domain. It is hard to remember now where the main convoy was bound except that it wasn't in the direction we should be heading. We were with them for quite a few days before peeling off to follow our ordered route to the Cape. As 1st Mate I took the 4–8 a.m. and p.m. watches. I was able, on occasions when conditions were favourable (i.e. fine weather with clear skies), to obtain positions by star sights at twilight. It seemed incredible that we, steaming at about 10 knots, should sail such a distance on our own without, as I remember, a scare. Navigation had to be precise for we followed a route devised for us before breaking off from the westward-bound convoy. At one stage we reached 49°W and could have been bound for Brazil and not South Africa. Many ships had been lost in these waters so we were constantly on the alert. There were double lookouts day and night and we were blacked out and showed no navigation lights during the hours of darkness. On a clear day the slightest wisp of smoke or the top of a mast showing above the horizon would mean a rapid alteration of course until we found ourselves in our own circle of water surrounded by the horizon. Then we would get back on to our specified route. At times it seemed as if we were not involved in the war.

As we sailed further south and the weather became warmer it was decided that we needed a swimming pool. The stores that the Canadian shipyard had put on board were quite incredible. The holds were secured by hatch beams, hatch boards and tarpaulins but, apart from spare tarpaulins, there were bolts of very good duck canvas, the best there could be. Anyone who could handle a sail needle and palm was put to work. Some who had never seen a palm and needle volunteered and accepted the blisters. The ship's carpenter made the framework with the spare hatch boards. The water was fed in from the deck wash line and the pool could be emptied through a small length of canvas hose leading from one bottom corner and tied at the top of the frame. It was a great success. Now, heading in a south-easterly direction, good progress was made with fine weather conditions.

There was one blot on our serene voyage. The assistant steward became very ill. He had a high fever with chills and was breathing rapidly. I was the self-appointed person in charge of the medicine locker which contained, as well as the usual pills, lotions, potions, bandages and splints, a small cabinet marked POISONS (dangerous drugs). There was also a book called *The Ship Captain's Medical Guide*. I held the keys to both the medical locker and the drugs cabinet. The patient was put to bed in a small cabin we had as a hospital. When putting him in bed with the help of the Chief Steward, I saw that his right knee was very swollen and looked inflamed. I saw the patient again at 8 o'clock that same evening when I came off watch. He looked very distressed and the knee was even more swollen. I could find

The Grand Priory in the British Realm of
The Venerable Order of the Hospital of St. John of Jerusalem.

AMBULANCE DEPARTMENT.

The St. John Ambulance Association.

Name of Candidate *Ronald F. Mc Brearty*

Rank in the Merchant Service

Home Address of Candidate (if any)

CERTIFICATE OF ATTENDANCE AT LECTURES.

No. of Lectures as per Paper 58	Place of Attendance at Lecture.	Date of Lecture.	Signature of Surgeon-Instructor.
1		12 FEB 1936	
2	MERSEY MISSION SEAMEN'S INSTITUTE, HANOVER STREET, LIVERPOOL.	13 FEB 1936	
3		14 FEB 1936	
4		17 FEB 1936	
5		18 FEB 1936	
6		19 FEB 1936	

CERTIFICATE OF EXAMINATION.

This is to Certify that *Ronald F. Mc Brearty* has been examined by me at **MERSEY MISSION TO SEAMEN, LIVERPOOL** on the 20th day of *February* 1936 and has qualified to render First Aid to the Injured.

Signed *W. A. Burton.*

Surgeon Examiner.

Countersigned *Harold G. Martin*

Chief Secretary or Local Representative,
St. John Ambulance Association.

The Surgeon-Instructor and the Surgeon-Examiner are requested to read the instructions on the back hereof.

First Aid Certificate.

nothing in the medical guide to help me and we were bound to radio silence so could not ask for help or guidance. The situation was now serious and with the knee puffed up I sensed that something had to be released. The Chief Steward came in to help me turn the patient over on to his left side. Then, with the Chief Steward holding an enamel bowl I stuck a scalpel into the back of the knee. The pus literally poured out and the stench was foul. A small piece of gauze was put into the wound to keep it open to allow further drainage. The Captain rightly decided to head for the nearest port, which at this time was Walvis Bay in South West Africa. This had once been a German colony and was now controlled by the British, but most of the white inhabitants were German speaking. We were there after a couple of days steaming and the assistant steward was landed and taken to hospital. He could possibly have developed septicaemia and died so a good job was done. But what if the scalpel had severed some artery?

Before sitting for his first Certificate of Competency, which was that of 2nd Mate, every candidate when presenting his papers must first have obtained a First Aid Certificate. This was achieved by attending six short consecutive lectures with dates recorded, after which there was a verbal examination. If successful you received a small linen document signed by the examiner and a representative of the St. John's Ambulance Association, which stated that you were qualified 'to render First Aid to the injured'. These were the only instructions given to officers in the Merchant Navy at that time and even broached the subject of childbirth! Just six short lectures. No more. In my time the lectures were not even given in the Nautical College but in the Mission to Seamen during the evenings. In the examination for 1st Mate the document was just endorsed with no further instructions. This was the only qualification I ever had in my long career in the Merchant Navy. I have since set broken bones, could stitch wounds quite well, and later on became a dab hand with the needle when giving injections.

No shore leave was granted in Walvis Bay but because it was available we took on board coal bunkers. We were on our way again after a few hours and then sailed close inshore to Cape Town, about six hundred miles further south. Not much time spent there either: just the Captain ashore to receive further routing instructions and to report the happenings before and during our stay in Walvis Bay. Again no shore leave and soon we were on our way to Durban on the east coast. Here we topped up our coal bunkers to the maximum capacity. I had become engaged before leaving Manchester and intended to marry on my next leave. With the strict rationing of food at home I saw Durban as the answer to the problem of the reception, the wedding cake and so on. I bought quantities of dried fruit, sugar, tinned fruit, anything I could think of. I must have been the eternal optimist.

Before leaving Durban we loaded a small consignment of cargo to be discharged in Kossier, a small port in the Red Sea, before entering the Gulf of Suez. We must have left the UK with a full dead weight cargo and loaded to our marks with correct freeboard. There was, however, cubic space available in some of the hatches in the tween decks and in between the beams. I seem to remember that this cargo was in bags but am unsure of the contents. We did not enter Kossier but anchored off and discharged into lighters. Work went on throughout the night with the lighters, which were not very large, having to be towed into harbour, emptied and brought back alongside. Next morning we were on the last lap. Our passage through the Suez Canal was normal and just as I had known it in peace time. Further routing instructions were received in Port Said and so we entered the Mediterranean and sailed westwards to Alexandria. Our cargo was eagerly awaited, for it consisted mainly of stores. Discharging went ahead quite smoothly and soon we were to know our fate. We had come to the Mediterranean the long way round and it had taken time. Now we were here we were going to stay here for quite some time. Our role, with other vessels, was to supply our ground forces with stores and equipment as they moved further westwards in pursuit of the enemy.

* * *

The battle of El Alamein had taken place a couple of months before and our troops were advancing along the whole front. Consequently lines of communication were being extended daily and the obvious way to supply them in quantity was by sea. We carried everything they could possibly need, but the bulk of the cargoes seemed mostly to consist of ammunition, petrol and 100-octane fuel. But first we had to be made ready. The holds had to be swept out and prepared for the loading of vehicles when required. An extra 12-pounder anti-aircraft gun was fitted on the fo'c'sle head just forward of the windlass. As 1st Mate my station when entering or leaving port was on the foc's'le head in charge of mooring, unmooring and anchoring. The gun platform was constructed so as to be high enough to clear bulwarks, anchor chains etc.; it also extended forward of the bow. I used to stand in the gun platform entering port in order to see all that was happening around my end of the ship and to be clearly seen from the bridge with which there was communication. The effect of this was that I was always the first to enter port. If entering through a breakwater I could look at the stem and see the ship following me.

Alexandria was now our home port. We loaded there on every trip except one when we went through the canal to Suez. Anyone who has been in these parts will remember the activities of a certain portion of the population to cheat, abuse, rob and mug any unsuspecting member of the forces. I wondered how they would have behaved had General Rommel taken over; I got the impression at times that they would have preferred it. We were warned, if alone, never to get into a taxi with a driver and another person alongside of him, but to make sure there was always only one driver. The only means of getting back to our loading berth, the Timbers Quays, was by taxi. Returning one night I took a taxi and was careful to note just one driver. I was fooled, however, for after a short distance he slowed down and another chap jumped in. I was very apprehensive and was ready to jump out the moment we stopped outside the dock gates. The taxi came to a halt a little way from the gate and as I got out so did they and stood each side of me demanding an extortionate fare. Fortunately, this was witnessed by the guard at the gate who was no doubt puzzled as to why the car parked so far away. He sensed something was wrong and came charging over with his rifle at the ready. With that the two leapt back into the taxi and sped off at speed. I hadn't paid a button. The guard was a Sikh. This was not the first time that I had had the assistance and protection of a Sikh who were the policemen in many British outposts and could be called the Custodians of the Empire.

One other story about a Sikh was when we were loading in Suez. Alongside the ship was a stack of ammunitions waiting to be taken on board. It was guarded by a Sikh soldier who stood impassively at ease with his rifle at his side. Some young Arabs were dancing round him, taunting him and making fun of his turban and beard. Eventually one of them overstepped the mark and came too near. Without much movement the soldier nearly knocked his head off with the butt of his rifle. He then resumed his position looking straight ahead. Cruel? Yes, but very effective.

There were more subtle ways of cheating. Like the baggy-trousered gent who came on board and showed me a note supposedly from the Ministry to say that our fresh drinking water tanks needed cleaning and he was the contractor assigned to do the work. I didn't check the source of the note which turned out to be a forgery. Since I had signed to say that the tanks had been cleaned he would be paid. On coal-burning ships like the *Fort Maurepas* the stokehold fires were cleaned and raked at the end of each watch. The ashes and clinker were then sent up in a steam operated tub or bin to deck where they were tipped into a large pipe called the ash chute which led out through the ship's side above the water line. Thus the ashes were disposed of. This method of disposal could not however be used in port; instead, the ashes were sent up and then wheeled by barrow to a place on deck where they were piled up until an opportunity arose to shovel them overboard. One morning there was a polite tap on my cabin door. Then there was the ingratiating introduction and inquiry as to my state of health. The purpose of the visit? Yes, he was another one. This time he had a contract drawn up and ready for me to sign. Again he had been sent by some Ministry official and he would be responsible for keeping the deck clear and would remove the ashes daily. I should have known that this was another fiddle. Just imagine the cost of a barge and small tug each day when we were in port! Thinking hard about this and what I had let myself in for, I sent for him and asked to see the contract again on the pretext that there was some line I had missed. He handed it to me whereupon I tore it up into pieces and felt much better. I was learning. Afterwards I was always suspicious of anyone bearing notes of authority from ashore.

Anyone sailing through the Canal before the war will

remember the tactics of the types who boarded ships with all sorts of junk for sale whilst they were waiting for transit through the canal at Port Said. They were a wily bunch of rogues but there was no malice and there was lots of good humour. I remember a young apprentice parting with a beautiful pure wool rug his mother had given him in exchange for a box of Turkish delight. One regular boarder called himself 'Sandy MacTavish' or 'Sandy McNab' and he had developed a perfect Scottish accent. It wasn't unusual in those days to see redheads. British troops had been around those parts for many years. Could this be the explanation?

To carry grain cargoes in British ships it was necessary to comply with what was known as 'The Regulations for the carriage of grain' and they had to be strictly complied with. To prevent the grain shifting, wooden bulkheads had to be erected in each hold running fore and aft and these had to be shored up to the ship side with large balks of timber. Most tramp ships carried these 'shifting boards' with them in case they were offered a grain cargo. A lot of timber was required to fit this safety measure and it took hours of hard labour for the crew to fit, as I well know. I mention all this because the *Fort Maurepas* had been well supplied before embarking on her maiden voyage from Vancouver. It was with some surprise that I received an authentic message, delivered by a uniformed dispatch rider, requesting (ordering) that I land all the timber. We were not likely to carry grain in the present circumstances, but the vessel could survive the war. It was not for me to question why it was taken off, but what happened to it? Was the native Alexandria bug affecting others?

After all these years it is not possible to record chronologically the various voyages made whilst I was in this theatre of the war, but there are many incidents which are still fresh in my mind. The 100-octane spirit was carried in forty-gallon drums and these were stowed in the bottom of the lower holds. Ammunition was next and then anything and everything that was required by the various units, including at times vehicles on the deck. The drums were not always handled with the care they deserved, the consequence of which was that there were many leakages and the petroleum vapour, which was heavier than air, would be locked in the bilges. It could be smelt on deck and could be quite dangerous. A system was devised to get rid of the vapour. It consisted of a pipe led down to the after bilge bay of each hold on port and starboard sides which was connected to the main deck steam line which fed the deck machinery. Another pipe led over the ship's side. As the steam ran across the open bilge pipe and to its outlet over the side it drew the vapour up and dispersed it. A marine engineer could explain this much better than myself. But it did work and was called a 'steam ejector'. The ejectors were turned on early each morning and late each evening. Other ships of our type were similarly fitted and it was quite a sight to see steam coming from so many places. There was still quite a lot of submarine activity in these parts and if they had been fitted with a smelling device on their periscopes they would have located us quite easily.

The planning of these trips by the Transport Officers was excellent. They were responsible for stowage plans and the organising and control of the dock labour. They were almost all ex-Merchant Navy senior officers now in the Royal Navy Reserve. We sailed in escorted convoys which were very small compared to what I had been used to in the North Atlantic. One

Transport Officer told me that since we were similar types of vessels we were each loaded with pretty much the same cargo, except, of course, the items consigned to special units. It meant that if any ships were sunk it would not disrupt the supply completely. This carrying of anything and everything down the line included, of course, NAAFI stores, cases of canned beer and cigarettes. There was a free issue of cigarettes, called Victory V, but no one would surely have paid for them. A strict watch had to be kept on the items in case they found their way into the wrong hands.

This running up and down the North African coast could be tedious and very often hazardous. The crew were generally very good, but one evening when checking up to see that all hands were on board, I found that one seaman had gone missing; in fact, he had deserted, taking his belongings with him. He was reported and, no doubt, would have been picked up somewhere, but we never heard any more about him. He was the only one during our spell in the Mediterranean.

The youngest of the coal trimmers on board found that he could not carry on doing this particular job which was feeding the coal in the bunkers down to the firemen in the stokehold to shovel into the furnaces. He was, in fact, scared of being trapped in the confined space of the coal bunker in the event of a submarine attack. He asked if he could be demoted to the rating of galley boy, whose only task was to peel potatoes, clean the galley and make tea for the ship's cook. His was the least important job of all the ratings and was the lowest paid. His was the last signature on the Articles of Agreement, signed before the commencement of the voyage. The galley boy, who was not really a boy, having gone over the age for that rating, was only too happy to change. It meant a lot more money for him and the trimmer would now spend most of his time handling a potato peeler instead of a shovel. I must confess to having a little sympathy for the trimmer if fear had really taken over. I would not have cared much for being caught down there in an attack. I had done a spell of trimming when I was an apprentice some years before, on a run between Japan and Java when crew were missing. I remember that you had to be eighteen years of age to take on the work, and if under eighteen there had to be two persons. At that time there was no fear of attack and it was a dirty job but I found it to be easier than my lot on the trampship I was serving on. The trimmer worked four hours on and eight hours off whereas I as an apprentice worked watch and watch, four hours on and four hours off. It is well known that some members of the Merchant Navy returned to sea after being torpedoed and sunk four and even more times and many of them served in the engine room and stokehold.

One other crew incident which at times causes a little pang of conscience, concerns one of the stokehold firemen. I had heard stories of fighting rum being given to the troops during the 1914–18 war but did not think it could happen now. However, there was some very strong rum which we took down the coast on one particular voyage. It was contained in all sorts of different bottles, whisky, lemonade, beer, all types with a cork banged in. About a dozen bottles were placed in a large tin container which had the top edges hammered over to form the lid. This fireman had somehow got hold of a bottle or two of this powerful potion and had now become most violent. He was not keeping his watch and on this particular afternoon came staggering into the officers' quarters bawling and shouting abuse. I was off watch and lying down on my settee, having what was called a 'one to three'. I assumed the Captain would be doing the same in his cabin above me. Next, I could hear more shouting and scuffling. The Captain had been aroused by the noise and had come down to the saloon where the fireman was now attacking him. I rushed into the saloon and between the two of us we managed to subdue him. He was a big man and completely out of control.

Next is the part I wanted to forget. My cabin was only yards away so I dashed in and came back with a pair of handcuffs. After we had managed to get them on behind his back we closed both saloon doors and laid into him until he was completely subdued and lying down. Not a nice thing to do, but he was a threat to the whole ship. After a while, with help from others, we took him forward where I handcuffed him to the ladder of the lower fore peak stores and left him. After a few hours he was released and was very sheepish and quiet. There were contingencies made for any serious breach of discipline on a British merchant vessel other than that which could be dealt with by the Master under the Merchant Shipping Act, and there was a Naval Court for this purpose. When we arrived back in Alexandria the incident was reported. He was removed from the ship, tried and, I presume, locked up.

Tripoli became our main port of discharge and once, after arriving, we were told that there was no shore labour available and we would have to remain at anchor. The following day the Senior Transport Officer boarded and enquired if the ship's Company would be prepared to discharge the cargo. Yes, was the answer and I was to be in control and organise the labour. The rigging of the derricks and the driving of the steam winches was work any seaman was familiar with. We did not carry deck ratings to form more than a couple of gangs or teams. Engineer officers, wireless officers, DEMS gunners, spare catering staff and engine room ratings were all persuaded or press-ganged to join in. There was an added attraction. There was to be a payment of so much an hour to be given by the Ministry. I suppose it came from the cash already assigned for the Arab workforce. A list of all the ship's personnel comprising the discharging gangs had to be kept together with the hours worked. This list of names was written at the end of each day by me, but there was one snag. Since I was the organiser and the person responsible for the whole operation, I was like the employer so did not figure on the roll for payment. I am sure we could have performed this task without any reward, but there it was and although I was doing more work than anyone else I was the only non-recipient. I thought long and hard about this and decided that a crew member named A. Brown should appear on each sheet. After a few days the dispute with shore labour was resolved and we were relieved and given our pin money. The crew were now able to look after the maintenance of the vessel.

Again in Tripoli, on another voyage, we were lying at anchor waiting for a berth. We had loaded a deck cargo of potatoes and onions. We hadn't been long at anchor when a small naval launch came alongside. A young RN Lieutenant presented himself. He was from a naval corvette lying at anchor a couple of hundred yards away. He had seen us come into the harbour and had noticed our deck cargo. They hadn't seen a potato on board for months and he wondered if he could buy a few sacks before we went alongside and they were carted away. I was feeling very charitable. After all, his vessel had probably been one of our escorts at some time. I asked him to take his craft to the other side away from any prying eyes ashore and take what he wanted. A little later he came back to thank me and then invited me to go aboard his HMS for a drink. He would come back for me in a couple of hours. I was all ready in my best whites when a boat came for me and I was soon in the wardroom with a large gin in my hand. After lots of pleasantries and re-charging of the glass an air-raid siren sounded. It was then immediate action stations and I was invited to the bridge to see 'our show'. Guns were blasting away. The 'all clear' came soon afterwards and we returned to the wardroom and resumed our previous activities. When the time came for me to be returned to my own vessel I noticed that the boat now to be used was larger and had more hands in it. There were now two officers and four ratings. To reciprocate their hospitality I invited the two officers for just a quick drink. It was now beginning to get dark and it was time for them to return to their own vessel, but as they pulled away I could see that the extra men had been busy loading the larger boat. There couldn't have been more than a couple of inches freeboard and she was down to the gunwales. Fortunately it was a calm and clear night and they arrived safely. I learned the next day that the air-raid had only been a practice and it seems that my host's vessel was the only one firing. The irony of this event is that I met those two officers months later in Malta and was able to tell them that from the time that we had met in Tripoli until the present time we had not had a potato on board. All we had been getting was sweet potatoes or yams. It hadn't crossed my mind to look after ourselves. I didn't think it was needed until a week later. The bags were not tallied on board and no doubt some would have found their way into the wrong hands.

Before leaving Alexandria on a run to Sfax No. 2 Hold tween decks was left empty. In the wings wooden bunks had been built for the whole length. They were more like shelves than bunks and were two or three tiers high. This was to be accommodation for prisoners of war on our return journey. I am not sure just how many we carried but all the allotted space was taken up. A hatchboard was removed from the after corner of each side of the hold and entry into tween deck was by means of a specially constructed wooden ladder on either side. The usual steel vertical ladder in the centre of the hatch remained covered. The prisoners were allowed on deck for exercise and fresh air at certain times of the day. They had guards with them and there were also our own DEMS gunners on board. We had been steaming eastwards without much activity but there were a couple of scares.

I was just coming to the end of my 4 a.m. to 8 a.m. watch at about 07.30. It was fine and clear with a calm sea. I happened to look aft and saw that the troopship *Yoma* had just been torpedoed. She was in another column in the convoy astern of us on our starboard quarter. She may have been hit by more than one torpedo for she had started to list. It was 7 June 1943 and the position was 33°03′N, 22°04′E. I called the Captain to the bridge and after appraising the situation it was decided that we would turn back and attempt to pick up some survivors. This was breaking all the rules of convoy discipline but it was impossible not to react after seeing the vessel listing and bodies in the water. The lifeboats were, as always when at sea, swung out and ready to lower into the water. Getting as close as we could the boats were launched. I took one and the 2nd Mate took the other. We had engines and were able to ferry survivors back to the *Fort Maurepas* and return to where there were others waiting to be picked up. Approaching some who were swimming around we came across one who had a large rat sitting on the life jacket around his shoulders: his own little Kapok island in the Mediterranean. If the rat expected to be given a new home he was wrong. A seaman in the bow took an oar and, putting it under the rat, threw it as far away as he could.

We were quite near to the *Yoma* and I was at first puzzled by the reluctance of some of the troops on the rails to jump into the sea. At this stage I had been at sea for twelve years and was very much at home on the water. I would have hated to have been in a land battle or among buildings being bombed. I was fortunate I was on my home ground and I had an advantage just like a football team playing at home. Yet I appreciated their feelings. For many it probably was their first journey abroad and they would never have seen such an expanse of water. It must have been terrifying. Scramble nets had been hung over each side just forward of the bridge. They were about 12' × 12' and made of 3" circumference rope and were lowered to the water making it easier to climb on board. A strange thing happened whilst we were trying to gather as many survivors as we could.

The senior ranking German prisoner was, I would think, equivalent to a warrant officer in the British Army. He spoke perfect English, as I had found when I had spoken to him about smoking in the hold. It was no wonder that he could speak English for he was from South West Africa, which had at one time been a Germany colony and was now what was called a British Protectorate. Apparently his German feelings were uppermost, and he had left South West Africa to join the German army. He asked the Captain if he and some of the men under him could man one of the small boats on the lower bridge and help in the saving of the survivors in the water. These boats did not have engines and would have to be rowed. He was given permission only on the understanding that a ship's gunner sat in the stern with a loaded rifle. They managed to pick up a few but soon an escort vessel arrived on the scene and we were ordered to rejoin the convoy which was now almost out of sight. They had to reduce speed drastically and wait for us to catch up. We had to give all the steam we could for if there were submarines about we would be easy pickings – a sitting duck. We eventually caught up with the convoy and assumed the rear position of one of the columns. During this rescue operation I witnessed a most remarkable sight. The whole of the ship's company, other than those on duty, were on deck and the German prisoners were among them. As the survivors were helped over the bulwark the prisoners wrapped a blanket around each one of them. It was their own blanket which had been issued when they came on board. It was a sight to remember. The crew organised a tarpaulin muster and provided dry clothing for the very wet survivors. Relationships between captors and captives became more relaxed.

Above the wheelhouse and covering the same area was what was called the 'Monkey Island'. It housed the ship's compass, used for plotting courses and taking bearings. It was surrounded on all sides by steel guardrails with three rungs about three feet high. It wasn't much protection from the elements for a navigating officer who had, at times, to climb up and down the ladder from the navigating bridge. It had long been my wish to have the 'Monkey Island' boarded all round to give some protection from the wind. I had collected the wood needed for the job but didn't have the labour. The answer lay with the prisoners. Talking to their WO one day, I asked if there were any carpenters among his men. Three were produced immediately and were set to work under the directions of the ship's carpenter. The prisoners were only too happy to be up there in the fresh air and in no time the job was completed. The cook did his best to feed the extra numbers but not all were content. There were a few French survivors and they were not too happy with the cuisine and said so; I thought at the time that they could have been a little more grateful. From a list made of the survivors I could see that they were from many different units, and had come out as replacements. The French would be Free French but I have no idea where they were bound. Although the British contingent were making the best of it, the French unit seemed very miserable.

We stopped off at the entrance to Alexandria just outside the breakwater where the survivors were taken ashore by craft sent out to meet us. Our destination was Port Said, a distance of 1,180 miles from Sfax where we had to land the prisoners. The British survivors thanked us as they left and each one handed back the clothing given by the crew to replace their soaking wet uniforms as their own clothing was by this time well aired and dry. This did not happen with the French who just disembarked and took what they had with them.

* * *

Some time later, when in Alexandria, we had our 4″ gun positioned on top of the poop deck housing aft replaced by a more modern version. The original was said to be of 1914–18 war vintage whereas this one was described as a LAHA – Low Angle High Angle. After fitting, trials had to take place outside the harbour. This new acquisition to our defensive armament made us quite a formidable force. At one time during our period in the Mediterranean we carried twenty DEMS gunners, one 4″, two 12-pounders and eight smaller AA guns.

Despite the reputation of Alexandria, a night ashore there was always welcome after a run down the coast. There was nowhere else we could go ashore at this time. When the opportunity arose I just frequented one bar which catered for ranks of sergeants and above. This particular bar suited me; I had been in other higher ranking establishments but the boyish behaviour of some of the officers after a few drinks did not appeal to me: things like playing rugby with a plant pot from the entrance. If this had happened elsewhere . . .

We were to sail at 8 o'clock next morning and I was free, sitting on a bar stool. I noticed two uniformed sergeants a few yards away. I was dressed in a lightweight grey suit which could be called, in those days, a Palm Beach suit. The sergeants kept looking at me and I was becoming uncomfortable. After a while they came over to where I was sitting and one of them patted me on the back. I wondered what next. But all was fine. They were two of the men I had picked up from the *Yoma* and they had recognised me. From then on it was just one big hectic night. They insisted that I go with them and be shown the town. Heaven knows where we didn't go. They were on leave and had a room in a small hotel and this is where we finished up. There were two beds and I was soon flat out on one of them. What made me stir I don't know, but at 6.30 I woke, realised where

I was and jumped up. I could hardly believe what I saw. Seated each side of a small table were my two benefactors with a large bottle of beer between them. Did I want more? Not likely. I was anxious to get back on board. The ship had been made ready for sea the night before but we still had to leave the berth at 8.00 a.m. as instructed, to form up outside the harbour. Anyone could be late coming on board but not the Chief Officer. I was getting worried and a taxi was all I needed and as soon as possible, this was then ordered. Shortly afterwards a tap came on the door. I thought, that's quick, and was ready to say my goodbyes and dash out. The driver could not be seen from where I was standing but the voice was clear enough. Not having seen a female taxi driver in Alexandria I thought it a little strange. Then one of the sergeants said, in a strong Scottish accent, 'Have ye time for it before ye go?' They had entertained me throughout the night and at no cost at all. Was this then the ultimate hospitality?

A taxi now arrived and I couldn't have cared less how many drivers it had, I was just so anxious to get back on board. So I thanked my new friends, bade them goodbye and was soon changing from my 'go ashore gear' into my uniform and preparing for sailing. Hopefully I would not meet any of the others in the same circumstances; one night like that was quite sufficient. Still, it was nice that my efforts had been appreciated.

Throughout the Mediterranean campaign, whenever headquarters were established in an occupied port, it seemed that the Royal Navy always commandeered the best building, not only for its strategic advantage, but also for prestige. After all, they were the senior service and as some of the best buildings or hotels were on the sea front, that is where they could operate their role controlling the harbour and shipping. This was the case in Tripoli after the occupation. 'Navy House' was soon established on the front. We had discharged our cargo and were lying at anchor in the harbour awaiting others to form up for the run back to Alexandria. A signal was received inviting the Captain and Chief Officer to the opening party of Navy House. We had to find our own way so a motor lifeboat was launched and brought round to the accommodation ladder. I am not very good with engines so a volunteer was needed to attend to the petrol engine should it be required. I would handle the tiller and find the landing which was quite a distance away. The 4th Engineer was the ideal man and he was only too pleased to have a run ashore.

When we arrived the party was in full swing and the place crowded. I understood that the officers had saved up their spirit rations for the occasion. There must have been some other means as well of acquiring the lotion for it was flowing freely. There was only one problem, a shortage of glasses. The bottoms of lemonade bottles had been cut off and made smooth by some means. Once you had got hold of any sort of receptacle the idea was to hold on to it. All you had to do then was to force your way to the bar, push it across and it would be dealt with. As the evening wore on some of the guests became more than merry. I had to steer our boat back in the dark through the harbour with many vessels at anchor, including a couple of RN destroyers, so had to be very careful. I became friendly towards the end with a Marine Major who had certainly been going the pace. The Captain came over from the company he was engaged with and indicated that he would not be returning on board that night but would be there in the morning. At this time the 4th Engineer was hovering around and it was time that we made a move. The 4th Engineer was a Scot and he and the Major were getting on well. I think he was also from over the border. When we decided it was time to depart the Major asked if we would give him a lift to a destroyer at anchor in the harbour. He knew which one to go to so we agreed. As we approached the vessel he was looking for, search lights were shone upon us and naval ratings, with rifles at the ready, were shouting and demanding who we were. Eventually we were allowed to draw alongside the port quarter which was the lowest freeboard deck. It was a bit difficult getting our friend on board. This was not the official gangway but just the lowest part of the vessel where we hoped to hand him over. The guard helped and we were able to heave him on board. We did not know it but this was not the last time that we would be in contact with the Major.

* * *

The following morning we set off to return to Alexandria to load. But this time it was for a new destination. The cargo was the usual mix of something and everything for various units with a bigger proportion of 100-octane and ammunitions. We were also to carry a contingent of troops. They formed a Royal Marine Anti-Aircraft Battery and were commanded by a Lt. J. Square. I mention him because he was a most remarkable character, a bit of a rebel and quite fearless, the sort of chap who you could imagine jumping out of a trench, pistol in hand, ready to kill as many of the enemy as possible. Certainly one who you would want on your side. We found a berth for him and his men camped on top of the hatches with spare tarpaulins spread over the derricks for shelter. The guns and trucks were stowed on deck. Lt. Square and his men arrived on board the evening before we sailed. Leave, of course, was cancelled but being in charge and making the rules he was the only one who could safely break them. With this in mind he invited me to go ashore with him for a drink or two. This was not meant to be a night out but just a few beers and a chat. He was in uniform but not the least concerned about whether he should be in this bar or that. We were not ashore for very long and I am sure enjoyed each other's company. We both knew that we were bound for Syracuse or at least that we were sailing to Sicily.

First we went to Malta and anchored outside Valleta Harbour to await other vessels and form up for our next trip which was to Syracuse only a short distance away, about seventy-five miles. The American forces had landed on the north shore of Sicily and the British on the eastern side. The ever efficient Lt. Square decided that his men should be made aware of the dangers of being torpedoed and what to do if this should ever happen. All this was in addition to the drills practised regularly on British merchant vessels. Lifeboats were lowered and pulled away from the ship side. We had no extra lifeboats to accommodate his contingent so he organised a 'jumping overboard drill'. I remembered well some of the troops on the *Yoma* who were so reluctant or scared to jump. If any of his men had the same feelings he was behind them to give them a push.

We weighed anchor and got under way at an appropriate time, in order to arrive off Syracuse at daybreak the next day. As we approached the harbour we were attacked by enemy planes. It wasn't a very sustained attack and there were no casualties, but it did bring us to attention after our smooth and quiet passage from Malta. Our land forces had consolidated their position and were in control of the port and pushing north. The initial landings had involved the LSTs, Landing Ship Tanks, which had been built in America from an original British idea. Over a hundred of them were transferred to the Royal Navy and their first operational role was the invasion of Sicily. They were built primarily for landing on beaches and were so constructed that their ballast arrangements made it possible to attain a forward draught of about three feet. They were the forerunners of the modern day roll-on roll-off car ferries with their huge bow doors and ramp. Before they arrived on the scene all vehicles: tanks, trucks, cars, anything on wheels, had to be loaded onto a vessel by means of a crane and slings specially adapted. These were loaded directly into the lower hold or stowed on deck, and depending on the height of the quay wall they were able to discharge directly onto the quayside. After the war they were used to bring back army equipment and personnel from the Continent to the UK. Later they were adapted to carry commercial vehicles and their drivers across the Irish Sea and the English Channel.

It must have been an awesome sight for the local Italian inhabitants to see the LSTs open their doors, lower the ramp and disgorge tanks and other weapons of destruction, the like of which they could never have imagined. It must have seemed like a chapter from Jules Verne or the Italian equivalent.

However, we were now in Syracuse and first had to discharge the Royal Marine Batteries' guns and trucks, and clear the hatch top where the marines had camped, so as to commence discharging our main cargo. I said my goodbyes to Lt. Square and we got on with the business in hand. There were intermittent air-raids at night and we had our usual action stations with our own AA guns manned and fire crews at the ready. I stationed myself in the wheelhouse and did regular rounds to all gun positions and fire fighting teams. One night the raids were a little prolonged and when the 'all clear' came the *Fort Maurepas* was still intact, but with just one casualty. The ship's carpenter running from one point to another had slipped and sprained his wrist.

In my earlier career the carriage of explosives demanded very special care. An explosives locker, or magazine to comply with the Merchant Shipping Act Rules, had to be built. This usually consisted of part of the tween deck or shelter deck in one of the holds being boarded-off right across the breadth of the ship. Steelwork had to be sheathed with wood and the steel deck covered with sawdust. It was entered through a door which, when not in use, was shut and padlocked. The picture in mind was of men in rubber shoes tiptoeing in and out carrying boxes of shells, ammunition or other explosives. It was a different story here in Syracuse. There was a sense of urgency to discharge and receive our cargo. Broken boxes did not cause any concern. Loose shells were just tipped onto the quayside. Every unit seemed most anxious to get hold of its consignment and I had frequent requests for this and that which was known to be on board. There was a cargo plan showing where the various items were but they were not always readily accessible. This did not seem to occur to one pushy and very rude sub-lieutenant who bounced on board and demanded that the cargo he had been sent to collect be off-loaded immediately. He did not get very far and was soon stamping down the gangway. Contrast this behaviour with that of a senior officer, a colonel who came on board. I was sitting at the desk in my cabin when there was a knock on the door. I invited whoever it was to come in. The colonel then entered and said, 'Good morning, sir; I wonder if you might be able to help me.' Whatever it was he had come for, it must have been vitally important or why would a senior rank be so concerned? After a chat and a drink I asked him to send someone down in the afternoon. With his description of the package and marks and numbers it was not hard to locate on the cargo plan. After a concerted effort involving the moving of other cargo his consignment was waiting on the quay. A little courtesy pays dividends!

During our time discharging cargo alongside the quay the 4th Engineer, who was off watch, went ashore and wandered into what was a restricted area. Word came that he had been picked up by the Military Police and would be detained. He must have gone some distance from the harbour for I stepped just outside the dock area without being apprehended. Some dwellings were badly knocked about and in one there were some holy pictures lying among the rubble just inside the entrance. I picked them up and they are still in my possession. However, back to the 4th Engineer who was to appear before the Provost-Marshal the following day. The Provost-Marshal was the officer responsible for law and order in any occupied area. There could never have been a coincidence quite like this for who should be the Provost-Marshal but the Major we had taken out to the destroyer after the Navy House party in Tripoli. It would seem that one good turn deserved another for our errant young engineer was delivered back on board without charge.

* * *

After completing unloading we went to an anchorage in the harbour to await others who would be accompanying us on the run back to Alexandria. Some ships had been hit whilst lying at anchor and were semi-submerged. Throughout my whole career in the Merchant Navy I had always had and had always met this feeling of pride in your ship. It did not matter how old the vessel was or if she was one of hundreds rolled off an assembly line, such as the Forts, Libertys, Empires or Parks; if you were on board then this was your ship and it should be better and be kept better than any of the others. There was no thought given to the fact that a well kept and painted ship was just as likely to be blown up and sunk as the rust bucket, so why waste the paint!

To make sure your ship looked better it was necessary to have a good supply of paint. So it was that one late afternoon we launched a motor lifeboat and set off for one of the wrecks. The sole object of this act of piracy was to see if there was any paint in the paint locker. We were fortunate and came back with a few five-gallon drums of the regulation grey. This success prompted us to repeat the operation whenever the opportunity arose in other invasion ports. We did not consider this looting. The accommodation was never entered and nothing was taken except stores and equipment to benefit our own vessel. After all we only took what the Ministry had paid for and we were working for the same firm.

Some time later on, when back in one of the North African ports, an Italian passenger ship had been sunk in the harbour. She lay on the bottom but most of the superstructure was above water. Signalling arrangements on the *Fort Maurepas* were most inadequate. Throughout the day there would be signal hoists from the Commodore vessel which had to be answered. And every ship at noon indicated her navigational position by hoisting a flag signal showing the observed latitude and longitude.

This meant two separate hoists of five flags. Most cargo ships had signal halyards on the foremast and also a stay from the foremast to the funnel to which was attached a number of blocks with halyards leading down to the navigating bridge. The *Fort Maurepas* had a signal mast on top of the wheelhouse with a sort of metal bar square fitted on the top. On each corner there was a block with signal halyards leading down. The flag signals were all too close and would get wrapped around each other. On British merchant ships there was only the officer of the watch and an apprentice to deal with any signalling required and this arrangement made it most difficult.

Into the picture now comes the Italian passenger ship. It was noticed that she had a long signalling yard attached to her upper foremast, bolted to the foremast with iron clamps. This was what was needed so we set off to board her but this time with additional hands and tools such as marline spikes, hacksaws, spanners and hammers, and also our own heavier wooden block and 3″ rope for lowering the yard down to the deck if we could detach it. It was very heavy, having had dozens of coats of paint. It was also too large to go in the boat but it was wooden and we took a chance and dropped it overboard. It was some time before it surfaced and even then was only just visible. Then the yard was towed back to our vessel and hauled on board. The engineers helped by altering the clamps to fit our own signal mast and the contraption on top was removed. In the meantime chipping hammers, scrapers and blow torches were put to use to remove the accumulated paint. What a difference it made when put in place. It was possible to raise flags from almost the wing of the bridge on each side. Just before leaving the Italian vessel I opened a door on deck which led down to the engine room and there, way below, sitting on top of the main engine casing, was a large bomb. Unexploded, I presumed, and so made a hasty retreat.

Air attacks were usually at night but one day we had an unexpected surprise. Early one morning on a fine clear day the sun had risen and was gaining height and strength. There was a breeze from the east. Lying at anchor, all ships would be facing eastwards which was towards the breakwater. There was a roar and without any warning two planes, flying very low, came in with the bright sunlight behind them and seemed to hop over the breakwater before letting go their bombs. They took everyone by surprise, including harbour batteries and ships' guns. It was over before any action could be taken and the two fighter bombers screamed away towards the north, climbing steeply. One of the ships at anchor was hit and sunk but there was no other serious damage. The next morning, with similar weather and conditions, every anti-aircraft gun in the harbour and on the ships at anchor was manned and waiting, but I did not expect that anyone would attempt such an attack again. But sure enough, at around the same time and with the glare of the sun behind them, there came the roar of planes approaching. They did not get very far this time for with all guns pointing towards them they were blasted out of the sky and fell the other side of the harbour. There were no casualties – not on our side at any rate. You wouldn't have thought that anyone could have attempted a second raid so soon afterwards. Surely they must have expected a different reception. We heard that the planes were Italian; perhaps that explains it.

We sailed shortly afterwards with the others in our convoy for Alexandria with a brief stop at Malta at anchor in the outer harbour. Loading in Alexandria was quick and we were soon on our way back to Sicily but this time further up the coast to Catania. We also had some troops on board, camping as before on the hatch tops with tarpaulins stretched across the derricks for shelter. I was a little concerned about smoking on the hatch top. The tarpaulins might have been burned and holed and would not have been waterproof. I was assured that all precautions would be taken such as buckets of sand. Whilst looking around I met and talked with a sergeant who came from Chester, my home town. We knew each other for we had been at the same school together when I was a boy of about thirteen. During the sea passage we recalled old times and people we both knew at the present time. He didn't say where he was going after disembarking, I don't suppose he even knew, but before saying goodbye he asked me if I could do him a favour. He was now a married man and wanted me to take some letters to his wife and family in Chester. Maybe he thought he would not get back and that I would be sailing home to the UK. He was taking a chance on me getting home safely. When eventually I did get back to Chester I took the parcel of mail round to the given address, only to find that he had been home and was now posted somewhere else. He had beaten me to it. I had, however, completed my mission successfully and like him was a survivor.

All mail was censored and any sent to me had to be addressed with name, rank, name of ship, c/o GPO, London. Any letters I sent, although addressed with name, street and town, were first censored wherever handed in and then sent to the GPO. Delays were inevitable and could be very long. The easiest and lightest type of letter being used was what was called an air mail letter form. This was a lightweight sheet of paper on one side of which you wrote, then it was folded and stuck down with pre-gummed edges to form a conventional letter shape. I once received twenty-three of these air mail letters in one delivery. They were from my fiancée whom I thought had forgotten me. I opened each one, placed them in the order they had been written, then, when a suitable time came for me to retire to my bunk, I just lay back and read the book, chapter by chapter. I had managed to convey to my parents which field of the war I was engaged in. I met a warrant officer in the Cheshire Regiment whose headquarters were in Chester. He had written to a friend who happened to know my father, and just mentioned that he had met me. No censorship was needed for he was known to have been in this area for a long time.

It was during this stay in Sicily that I had the misfortune to have a severe attack of toothache. It was really very painful and was interfering with my normal duties. As the officer in charge of the medicine locker I sought solace there. Looking through *The Ship Captain's Medical Guide* I found this entry under 'Toothache': 'The tooth should be stopped or, if too far gone, removed on the first available opportunity.' A lot of comfort this would be if in the middle of the Pacific Ocean. 'In the meantime, a piece of cotton wool dipped in creosote and pressed into the cavity often gives relief.' Mine was really raging and as we were in port arrangements were made for me to have treatment ashore. I was taken by army truck some miles out of town to what would be called a field hospital. There the offending molar was removed and another tooth showing signs of wear was drilled and then filled. The drilling was done with a mechanical hand-drill, and the filling remained intact for many years. I had had this sort of treatment before the war in Shanghai where the dentist came on board with his drill and a contraption like a spinning wheel; those fillings were also very successful. I was very pleased to have had this treatment here instead of having to suffer until we arrived back in Alexandria.

When there, it was decided that we go into dry dock for what used to be called a 'wash and brush up'. We were beginning to lose a little speed owing to barnacles and grass weed which attached themselves to the underwater plates of the vessel. It was quite some time since she had been commissioned in Vancouver. The underwater part of the hull had to be cleaned by means of scrapers, brushes and water jets and, when dry, painted with the appropriate type of paint. This consisted of a first coat of anti-corrosive paint, then a coat of anti-fouling paint to discourage the limpets and grass weed from becoming attached. If ships' bottoms were not scraped and cleaned the marine growth caused a lack of speed. A lot of paint was needed and this was supplied in ten-gallon drums. The order was placed and the paint drums were sitting on the dry dock bottom ready for use. Before this operation commenced I went down the dry dock steps to count the number of drums and to make sure the correct number had been delivered. All was well as the dockyard foreman and I counted the drums. After walking round to the other side of the vessel I came back to my starting point which was near the ladder or steps. Before ascending I happened to put my hand on one of the drums. It was empty. During my walk out of sight empty drums had been substituted for full ones. I should have known what to expect. We were in Alexandria and this was just another example of the devious, cheating style of life which seemed to manifest itself at every level.

Out of dry dock and operational again, we were ready for our

Ship discharging equipment and stores in landing craft (LCTs) as happened during the African, Sicily and Italian campaigns. (Imperial War Museum.)

next cargo. The Allied forces were now on the mainland of Italy and pushing north. Our contribution was to bring the supplies they needed. Loading went on throughout the night. The deck officers were on duty at all times to supervise the loading and arrange for the ship's derricks to be raised or lowered depending upon where in the hold the cargo had to be loaded. At times the handling of the derricks had to be done by the officers themselves as it would have been dangerous to leave it in the hands of some of the Arab labour employed. This cargo was not very much different from the many others we had carried except that the decks were covered with transport vehicles of all shapes and sizes. We again had troops camping on top of the hatches and these were the drivers of the trucks and cars. We worked long hours with no sleep and still had to pick up our sea watches as soon as we left port. This is just an observation. There were many others in this area having a much harder time than us.

Our destination was the Italian mainland and later instructions were to proceed to the Gulf of Salerno where both British and American troops had made a beach landing. Arriving off the Salerno beaches we anchored and prepared to discharge our cargo. This was to be done by off-loading into landing craft which were soon alongside. These were not the large LSTs but a much smaller version with an open section from the engine room bulkhead aft to the landing ramp in the bow. They were very shallow draughted and could run up onto a beach, but not shallow enough to prevent the vehicles having to complete their journey with their wheels in the water. There was some anomaly about these craft which made them very difficult to manoeuvre. I think it was that they were twin screw vessels but both propellers revolved in the same direction. The troops accompanying the vehicles were from a transport unit and we learned that they were recruited from Jewish volunteers from various parts of Eastern Europe. They were not combatant troops and did not appear to be armed.

The word 'condom' is commonly used today. Its use and function is spoken of freely. It is advertised in newspapers and magazines. It is not only shown on television but there have been programmes with explicit instructions as to its use. You could be led into believing that this was some new contraption, something newly invented. But long before the war this product was freely available at chemist's shops, although not on display, and was marketed under a different name which I will not repeat for fear of offending one of our European neighbours. I was about to learn that it also had other uses. The deck cargo of vehicles was obviously the first cargo to be discharged so as to leave clearance for the hatchboards and beams to be landed allowing access to the holds. Before this operation took place I saw a British sergeant who I assumed was in charge of the unit instructing the drivers as to how they should drive off the landing craft and onto the beach, taking into account that the last few yards would be through the water. The engines were all exposed with bonnets held up. Alongside him he had a carton full of the rubber protectives and was demonstrating how to fit them over the battery cell caps. The teats were pricked with a pin to allow any gas to escape. The terminals were smothered in grease and wrapped in tape.

* * *

The German forces were lodged in the hills overlooking Salerno Bay and were intermittently shelling the anchorage. A Royal

Navy cruiser was lying a little off our starboard side and was returning the fire and silencing them. After a while it would start again. It was good to see our side in action but it was not very good on my ears. I hated noise. It is not so bad when you are doing the firing, for then you know when the bang is coming. One morning, when I was on a routine inspection of cargo gear, one of the seamen asked me to go down into the crew's quarters below the poop deck. He showed me into the cabin he shared with another seaman and in the hull plating on the ship's side away from the two-tiered bunks was a jagged hole. The penetration must have been made by shrapnel and this prompted a thorough inspection of the whole of the hull which was best done from the inside. A number of similar holes were found, on the starboard side only. The control vessel HMS *Hilary*, an ex-Booth Line passenger vessel, was informed but did not offer much of a solution. Cement boxes could have been fitted by the ship's personnel but we would probably then need more cement and sand. American forces however had landed on the beaches about ten miles south of us and a message must have been passed to them for, early next morning, a large salvage tug came alongside. It was equipped to perform many functions, towing, fire fighting, pumping out tanks. It also had divers on board and welding plants. In no time stages were rigged over the side and the American welders set to work and with small steel plates of all shapes and sizes welded patches on each of the holes. Soon we were seaworthy again. It was all highly efficient and proved to me that they were well ahead of us in their thinking of what might be required in circumstances like this. Never mind the banter about the American forces having one supply ship filled with Coca Cola and another with ice cream, they really were able to handle most situations of this nature. Later on I will tell you of another incident which manifested their efficiency when we were discharging equipment for them in Naples.

As the land battle moved further north so we were ordered to sail up the coast to a new anchorage. It was thought to be a good idea to take the landing craft moored alongside with us instead of them having to follow on much more slowly speed. With extra moorings securing the craft we set off at a moderate speed. All went well until a craft alongside the afterdeck parted or slipped one of its mooring wires. Unfortunately the wire became foul of the ship's propeller. We stopped and immediately commenced filling our forward ballast tanks in order to raise the stern as much as possible. On inspection it was found that the wire was only wrapped around the propeller blades and not hard up against the stern tube, but it meant repeated diving attempts to throw the wire clear. Only a little could be done at a time and then you would have to come up for air. The wire was cleared and I had many lacerations on my body and arms as each time I went down, I was in contact with the stern frame. With this operation completed we were able to proceed whilst at the same time pumping out the forward ballast water. It was very pleasing to have been able to have cleared the wire from the propeller without having to have called again for the assistance of the American salvage tug.

After completion of discharge we were ordered back to Alexandria, again via Malta. Whilst at anchor off Valleta harbour, I was overjoyed to witness the surrender of a large part of the Italian Navy. Any opposition from the Italian forces had collapsed and an armistice had been granted. Some of the fleet had been sunk by German bombers to prevent them falling into

Allied hands but these vessels sailed, rather pathetically it seemed, in line ahead into Valleta Harbour.

* * *

We returned to Alexandria and made further voyages along the North African coast, going further west on each occasion.

I don't know how or why this came about but after one discharge, instead of returning eastwards we sailed for Gibraltar. Our vessel was either superfluous to requirements or we were being relieved. We had been away for eleven months, and expectations were high that we would sail across the Atlantic to the USA, load for the UK and go home. Arriving in Gibraltar, we were ordered to anchor in the bay. This put paid to any ideas some might have had of having a night ashore among much better company than that which we had had to endure during these last months. Any such things as alcoholic beverages were just a memory at this stage of our voyage so most were relieved to learn that the Captain had managed to twist the arm of those in control on the Rock and it was agreed that half the crew could have shore leave from 10.00 a.m. to 6.00 p.m. and the other half on the following day. A launch was engaged to ferry those who wished to stretch their legs ashore. You could feel very cooped up after weeks of nowhere to go and all of the ship's personnel took advantage of the offer. Those left on board were not completely denied any chance to celebrate the fact that we might now be homeward bound. Small boats came out to offer cheap trinkets and presents to take home and a limited supply of the amber liquid. There were no absentees when the return launch arrived alongside. Security was and had to be very strict and any defaulters would have soon been rounded up. Those who went ashore were able to indulge in the delights of drinking a glass of beer in an establishment which was the nearest they had seen to a British pub for many a long time.

During this spell at anchor we had on board a group of Royal Navy divers who swam underneath the hull from stem to stern and particularly along the bilge keel, feeling for limpet mines which had been found attached to other vessels by frogmen operating from the Spanish port of Algeciras, lying across the bay a short distance away. It was now winter and the Atlantic current flowing into the Mediterranean made the water very cold. The divers were always sure of a hot drink when they came back on board. Spain at this time was supposedly a neutral country but it was well known that some of their Atlantic ports harboured supply vessels for the German U-Boats.

General Franco was the supreme ruler of Spain so it was not surprising that although Spain had proclaimed her neutrality there would be bias towards the German–Italian alliance. After all, hadn't they helped him to gain control of Spain in the Civil War of 1936 by the use of German planes and naval craft?

After replenishing our coal bunkers from one of the hulks lying at anchor near us we set sail for our new destination. Sadly, it was not to proceed to the UK but to go south after leaving the Straits of Gibraltar. We were bound for Freetown in Sierre Leone, a distance of just over 2,000 miles, where we were to load a full cargo of iron ore. U-Boat activity had slackened off in this part of the Atlantic and we had an uneventful passage down the West African coast. There were a few ships anchored off Freetown but we were destined to load a little way up a fast flowing river where we berthed alongside a jetty. The loading was by means of a chute and consequently the vessel had to be moved up and down the jetty. It was, however, reasonably quick and we were soon down river again where we joined other ships to form a small convoy and headed north again. This was the second cargo of iron ore that I had carried during the war. Our heavy industries were dependent on its import and we were carrying a most essential cargo. Not one of the best cargoes, if you were thinking of your own safety. A conventional cargo ship or general trader would need less than half of the available cargo space to load a full deadweight cargo because of the weight of the ore which would occupy only 15–20 cubic feet for each ton. Consequently, if torpedoed, there would be a rapid influx of sea-water into the empty space and with the vessel already down to her marks, she could sink in minutes, sometimes without giving the crew a chance to launch their lifeboats.

We knew when leaving Freetown that we were bound for London, a distance of 3,000 miles if following a direct route. But this was not possible and apart from any extra mileage due to alterations to avoid the U-Boats, we still had to sail round the north of Scotland and through the Pentland Firth, then down the east coast. We had joined up with others who had left Gibraltar and some of these ships were bound for west coast ports so our first stop was Loch Ewe in Scotland. Then in convoy again we went to Methil in the Firth of Forth and finally made the hazardous run down the east coast among the colliers and coasters who had been running this gauntlet for so long. After passing the anti-aircraft forts in the Thames Estuary we sailed through the boom defence gateway and were now home and dry.

We were bound for London but not quite, for we berthed at the Ford Motor Works jetty at Dagenham. As I remember it they had their own foundry at that time. It was a long hike from the jetty to Dagenham itself or to any thoroughfare or sign of habitation, especially during the night when everything was blacked out. I had been on the *Fort Maurepas* for fourteen months and a walk ashore, especially when it meant putting your feet on English soil again, seemed to be the most appropriate action to take. At the top of the road on a corner was the inevitable pub which did not have to do much beckoning. Opposite was the welcome sight of two very familiar red and glass structures, the British telephone kiosk. I was now able to tell my parents and my fiancée that I was safely back. A few of us who had met ashore ambled back in good spirits and before stepping on the jetty looked inside this huge complex where the night shift were hard at work. There was no disguising who we were and a foreman came up and asked us if we would like to avail ourselves of the facilities of their canteen. This we gladly accepted and we had coffee and sandwiches.

I had already decided that I would leave the *Fort Maurepas* and I intended to get married as planned when I first joined the vessel. There were quite a lot of things to pack, the most difficult being all the unrationed provisions I had bought in Durban on the way round to the Mediterranean. I got over this by putting it all in a rather large wooden box which was securely nailed down and addressed, using paint, to my parents' address, then taken by taxi to the nearest railway station and sent as freight. It took two of us to handle the box and the same applied when it arrived at my parents' home. When saying my goodbyes I thought how strange it is that you can just say 'Cheerio' after living in a very small community for fourteen months. I had done this before with white officers and native crews, Chinese, Indian, Malay, and for a longer period of twenty-two months.

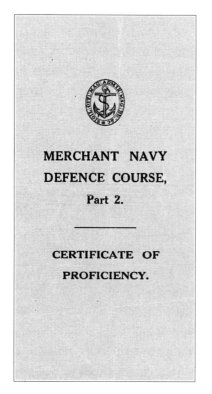

MERCHANT NAVY

DEFENCE COURSE,

Part 2.

———

CERTIFICATE OF

PROFICIENCY.

C.
MERCHANT NAVY DEFENCE COURSE
Part 2.

Name in full ...
(in block letters) McBREARTY. Ronald.

Usual Signature...

Grade and No. of
Board of Trade
Certificate   ... Master. 49216.   Year of Birth 1915.

	Date completed	Signature of Instructional Officer
SECTION I ...		
SECTION II	2 4 MAR 1944	

This Officer has completed Part 2 of the
Merchant Navy Defence Course and is considered
capable of taking charge of the Armament of a
Defensively Equipped Merchant Ship.

W. S. May,
Lieut. Commander, R.N.
for ~~Training Commander~~ Officer,

Port...

Date..........2 4 MAR 1944.............

Defence Course Part 2.

Stranger still is the fact that if you met one of these companions years later you would carry on talking as if you had seen each other a couple of weeks ago.

I had accrued thirty days' leave since leaving the UK and after twenty days at home I was married as arranged. This took place at 12.20 one Sunday and was followed by a six-day honeymoon in nearby North Wales.

On the completion of my leave I reported to the Merchant Navy Officers' Reserve Pool and was sent on another gunnery course. This was called Merchant Navy Defence Course Part 2 and consisted mainly of the firing of 4″ LA and HA guns and heavier anti-aircraft weapons. The instruction took place on a beach at Formby on the Lancashire coast near Southport. This was very convenient for, living in Chester, I was able to travel to and fro daily. I had had quite a bit of experience with guns, having earlier on in the war been in the 4″ gun crew and soon after been made Officer in Charge (uncertificated) by the Captain. But this was different. I was being taught by very experienced Royal Navy gunners and ended up with a Certificate of Proficiency which stated: 'This Officer has completed Part 2 of the Merchant Navy Defence Course and is considered capable of taking charge of the Armament of a Defensively Equipped Merchant Ship.'

Chapter 6

SS *Samwake*

Back now to the Officers' Pool. I was sent to Birkenhead for an interview with the Marine Superintendent of one of our oldest local passenger and cargo lines. I was offered the position of 2nd Mate with promotion guaranteed after one voyage. Pride then took over. It would mean stepping down a rank and removing one band from my uniform jacket. I had been Chief Officer for fourteen months and did not really like this idea. One voyage could mean any length of time and who knows if I would even return. If lost at sea the report would state 'R.F. McBrearty, 2nd Mate'. You were allowed to refuse one or maybe two appointments if agreed by the Officers' Pool. My next interview was in Liverpool for a position of Chief Officer in a company well known to me. They had vessels similar in size and style to the ones in which I had served as apprentice and 3rd Mate on round the world voyages from New York. I was very pleased to be accepted and no doubt they were happy to have someone who was familiar with their peace-time trade should the company and myself survive. Things were even better when I learned that I was to be sent to America to join a Liberty ship nearing completion. The Captain was already out there and in my care were the rest of the ship's Company.

The Mauretania as a troop-ship. (Imperial War Museum)

One day we assembled at the offices of the Reserve Pool and were taken by coach to the Prince's landing stage on the River Mersey. We boarded the *Mauritania*, one of the Cunard Line's largest passenger vessels. She was now engaged in ferrying troops to and from all theatres of the war. On this particular voyage most of the passengers were American Air Force personnel who were returning to the USA after completing an untold number of bombing missions over enemy territory. They had more than done their share and those who had survived the continuous onslaught were going back.

I have mentioned before my dislike for life on passenger ships or 'floating hotels' with their self-appointed organisers among the passengers who would hound you to take part in activities or to enter competitions. At this time, there were dozens of large liners carrying fare-paying passengers to virtually all the countries of the world. It was the main, and in most cases the only, means of travel across the seas. Each of the developed nations had its own fleet made up of various shipping companies each vying with others for business. First class travel on the better liners meant living in complete luxury. Ship cruises had started, but only in a limited way. Life aboard the *Mauritania* was very different. There were no parties, no games, no drinks. This last was because the US forces did not at that time allow alcohol on board their own vessels. We did, however, have some interesting talks and music. And don't believe the story that Coca Cola and aspirin make a good substitute.

The *Mauritania*, with her great speed, would obviously be sailing independently and not in convoy. There would be many diversions from the recognised route from Liverpool to New York but we were unaware of them, having no part at all in the running or navigation of the vessel. We were just passengers and were supposed to just lie about and relax. This was equally boring and I was not at all dismayed when I received a request from the Captain to take charge of a section of the boat deck during lifeboat drills. I was a Master Mariner and sailing as Chief Officer, so was an obvious choice to assist his own complement of officers. It was surprising how many of the pilots had difficulty in wearing the Board of Trade lifejackets provided. The old type of eight blocks of cork had been superseded and the new ones were secured in a different way. The drill gave me something to do and as it happened daily I was glad to help. After a couple of days out the Captain sent for me. I thought I was going to be rewarded with the hospitality generally envisaged when invited to this holy sanctuary. After all, I was of the same breed. But no, it was a complaint which was left for me to deal with. Some of the crew, mostly from Liverpool, had been gambling. They were taking money off the American lower ranks playing that 'only one can win game' Crown and Anchor.

On arrival in New York we were taken to hotels. Officers were accommodated in a very fine hotel right in the centre of the city. The crew stayed in a hotel nearer to the docks. The ship we had come to join was not yet completed and was being built in Portland in the state of Maine over three hundred miles to the north. We were well looked after during our stay in New York. The English Speaking Union were most interested in our welfare and arranged for tickets to be sent to our hotel for various stage shows. There was no war going on in New York and Broadway was still Broadway. There were also invitations to private homes which I was not too keen on, being quite happy to go along with my own colleagues who would converse and behave in a manner peculiar only to seafarers. I did, however, get inveigled into going with two others to a luncheon invitation in a very sumptuous apartment in Park Avenue, which I believe was the place to live. Our hosts were very kind and genuine but I cannot say that I enjoyed it and was glad in a way when we were heading 'down the avenue' to our temporary hotel room. It was entrusted to me to visit the crew and see if they were faring all right. The ship's agent would send a taxi to collect me and take me down to where they were staying. I would have cash with me so that those who needed it could have an advance of their wages. The Articles of Agreement had been signed before we left Liverpool and it was just as if they were on board ship, being given an advance of pay, duly signed for, so it could be deducted from the final balance of wages at the termination of the voyage.

After about a week enjoying the bright lights, we travelled up to Portland by train and again had to go into hotels as our vessel had not quite been made ready for sea. It was only for a couple of days and we spent this time in the storerooms of the shipyard checking essential equipment, stores and provisions, charts etc., which would later be on board in their appropriate places. Everything you might possibly need was there, the one exception being sextants which each deck officer had to provide himself. We boarded our new home in a body one afternoon and sailed a few hours later. After going full ahead, full astern, testing the steering gear and rudder, then dropping and re-stowing both anchors, we were away on passage. There was no returning to port with a list as long as your arm drawn up by the ship owners or managers/superintendents, of the defects to be rectified by the builders before final acceptance. And not, as far as I remember, a speed trial over a measured mile outside the harbour. No, it was 'here is your ship, take it away' and this is just what was done as we headed south for Boston to load for the UK.

The one thing that impressed me most after boarding was the attention that had been paid to detail in receiving us. Everything was in its place. Tools were where they belonged, the galley fires were lit, bunks were made up, soap and towels laid out. Yet there were still some painters finishing off in the alleyways. In my own cabin the standard officer-type rack to hold a water bottle and two glasses had been put in place and the bottle was filled with water. Unfortunately, they had not left anything to go with it. The 2nd Officer, now living in New Zealand, with whom I have been in touch recently, tells me that even the chartroom pencils had been sharpened.

The Liberty ship was a great improvement on the Fort ships. They were steam ships but oil fired and had many improvements. The accommodation was all in one block amidships in three tiers. Toilet arrangements were much improved with a number of shower cubicles which meant you never had to wait. There was also a laundry room, something I never imagined would be on a cargo vessel. The cargo handling gear was very good and another fine feature was their heavy lift or jumbo derricks. For conventional cargo ships I found this gear to be the most efficient I had worked with. The purchase lifting blocks were of five sheaves and worked on a sort of yo-yo principle, with both ends of the lifting wire going to separate winches. The wheelhouse had adequate instruments (no radar in those days) but had a very poor view for both the officer on watch and the helmsman. There were just three smallish windows in the forward steel bulkhead to see through. There was another means of steering by a wheel on the deck above, behind the standard compass called the Monkey Island, but this was open to the elements or anything else, with just steel rails surrounding it. The days of steel hatch covers had not yet arrived so it was the traditional hatch beams, hatch boards, tarpaulins, battens, wooden wedges and locking bars which made the vessel seaworthy.

It is not widely known that the Liberty ships were a British design but were built in the USA because of the abundance of materials and the safety of their shipyards which were free of air attacks and had no blackout.

The first Liberty ship, the *Patrick Henry*, was launched on 27 May 1941 in Baltimore. Hundreds more came down the slip-ways of the US shipyards on both west and east coasts, many to find an early watery grave.

The Liberty ship was, in my view, a very seaworthy and efficient vessel absolutely essential to the British and American merchant fleets if the Battle of the Atlantic was to be won. By this time 2,320 British merchant ships had been sunk and without these replacements all would have been lost. Records show that over 2,500 Liberty ships were built throughout the campaign. I have sailed in convoys of forty or fifty ships in which every one was a Liberty vessel. As well as being well founded they were, for merchant ships, quite well armed. The *Samwake* had a 12-pounder anti-aircraft gun on the fo'c'sle head, two Oerlikons on the fore deck, four Oerlikons on the mid-ship housing, one at each corner, and a 4″ LAHA gun on the poop house. Also on this deck were two more light anti-aircraft guns and a rocket launching device consisting of six rockets each side in racks. It was operated by a person inside a reinforced armed cubicle with controls to discharge the rockets together or separately. It could be angled any way and swivelled round in any direction. For a 'defensively equipped merchant ship' I think we were quite well equipped.

Liberty Ship Particulars

Tonnage	7,176 gross
	4,380 net
	10,865 deadweight
Length	442 feet
Breadth	57 feet
Draught	28 feet

During loading operations the crew were set to work on giving the hull another coat of paint. This may have seemed strange so soon after leaving the shipyard but I had no idea how many coats had been applied and took this opportunity to provide a further protective coat to that part of the vessel which would suffer most from the effects of wind and salt water when crossing the Atlantic. One morning I noticed that three seamen were missing from their place of work which was on the stages rigged for painting. I thought it was a case of absence without leave, a finable offence which would be dealt with when they eventually returned on board. Later on, when standing on the bridge, I picked up a pair of strong binoculars, intending to look at a ship on the opposite of the dock to see what sort of cargo it was loading. To my surprise it wasn't the cargo that caught my eye but there, working with the American stevedores, were my three missing crewmen. Being paid big money by the Americans would easily cover any monetary fine imposed on board. Two sources of income seemed to be a good idea but was brought to an end when I sent the 3rd Mate to round them up.

This eastern crossing was of the same pattern as the many others I had made before with a first leg up the US and Canadian coast to Bedford Basin in Halifax, Nova Scotia, there to join a large convoy homeward bound with miles and miles of extra distance to be sailed to avoid any potential U-Boat attack. First we went to Loch Ewe in western Scotland, then through the Pentland Firth and down to Methil in the Firth of Forth. A regrouping, then the bomb alley run to the Thames where we arrived safely with our own personal barrage balloon. At dawn one morning the skies were blackened by hundreds of Lancaster bombers returning from their nightly mission of destruction. To me, it was a comforting sight.

We had embarked two passengers before leaving the USA. One as I recall was Polish, perhaps a diplomat with whom I had very little contact. The other was Bertrand Russell, the famous English philosopher, broadcaster and author who wrote about politics, morals and science. He was a very interesting person and each night when I came off watch at 20.00 we would sit and talk until it was time for me to retire and rest before being called at 03.45. He was then seventy-two years of age and I believe had a very young American wife and child but this was not his first venture into matrimony. He was very alive and vigorous and also very good company.

The two passengers were to disembark whilst we were at anchor off Methil. I thought a pilot ladder over the side would be sufficient access for them to board the launch sent out to meet them and this was duly placed in position. This presented Earl Russell with no problems at all but the other gentleman decided he couldn't manage to go down the pilot ladder and insisted that we rig the accommodation ladder. This would mean unlashing the heavy stepped ladder, rigging bridles and chains, putting stanchions in their sockets and two lengths of guard ropes on either side. It would take some time and had we known he was going to be awkward it would have been rigged before we anchored. The vessel was fully laden so there was not a great distance from the deck to the waterline and the launch would be a few feet above that. As requested, this means of disembarking was provided, then much to my great pleasure and others watching, the sprightly Earl threw his leg over the gunwale and descended down the pilot ladder with his white hair flowing in the breeze. He turned and waved goodbye and was cheered by the crew. The other 'guest' walked slowly down the accommodation ladder to complete silence. He looked about twenty years younger than the Earl but was not as active.

* * *

When we arrived in London the invasion had already taken place. So also had Hitler started his retaliatory flying bomb attack on the capital. It was described as a flying bomb, being a pilotless craft with a warhead of some 1,800 lbs. It was christened the 'Doodle Bug' but was built as the V1 and later the V2. The principle was that when the fuel was exhausted the bomb dropped like a stone wherever it was at that time. When flying, it had a very distinctive and audible sound and could be seen especially at night by the jet flames from its tail, as if its rear was on fire. As soon as the noise stopped you knew it was on its way down and a run for the shelter was essential, then came the anxious wait whilst it hurtled down to cause more havoc, death and destruction. It was a fiendish weapon but this was total war. The first V1 was launched against London on 15 June 1944.

They could be seen heading towards London as we turned into the Thames Estuary. There were stories of heroic fighter pilots flying close alongside the V1 and attempting to flip the wings of the bomb with their own, and so alter its flight path and direct it to an unpopulated area or even into the English Channel.

My wife decided to brave the bombs and come down to London to see me. She booked into the Howard Hotel on the Embankment and I made my way there at night to spend a lot of the time in the air-raid shelter.

* * *

The cargo we had brought across the Atlantic from Boston was for use in the UK and had to be unloaded before we could ship the armoured car vehicles and other equipment needed on the other side of the Channel. Work went ahead smoothly and eventually we were able to lock out of the docks into the river and proceed downstream to a position off Southend, where the convoy was being assembled. Our decks were completely covered with vehicles, hardly a space anywhere, making it difficult to move about. Intermingled with the deck cargo was a contingent of troops who would be manning the vehicles and guns when we had landed them on the beaches. They camped where they could. The officer-in-charge, a Lieutenant Colonel as I remember, fared much better. He was offered the facilities of the ship's hospital, a small cabin with one bunk.

Up till now all ships in their grey livery were nameless. That is to say, they could not be identified by just observing them, although certain companies with distinctive hull shapes and size of funnels and masts would be known, but not the name of one particular vessel of the fleet. The convoy plan listing all ships and their positions named each vessel and gave certain particulars. All vessels crossing to Normandy were now obliged to display their name in large letters on a board attached to the Monkey Island rails on port and starboard sides. The name stood out, painted black on a white background, and was about two feet high. The reason for this departure from the 'no name' rule was to assist the beach masters and transport officers to identify vessels easily and to allocate anchorages or berths on the artificial breakwater. It made a lot of sense, especially with the number of ships of identical shape and size arriving with totally different cargoes, namely the Libertys.

We were proceeding steadily down river, when just off Ford's Works at Dagenham, a very strong and loud hailing system bellowed out, '*Samwake* ahoy, *Samwake* ahoy, *Samwake* ahoy,' and then 'Ford war workers wish you a safe passage and a speedy return.' This was well received and answered with blasts on the ship's whistle. This gesture from the Ford Plant was very much appreciated.

We anchored off Southend and the Captain went ashore to attend the Convoy Conference with the Commodore, Escort Commanders and other ship masters involved. After the briefing we sailed in single file through the deep water channels of the Thames Estuary, avoiding the many sandbanks, until we could form up in the downs off Dover, where we again witnessed the frightening spectacle of the deadly flying bombs which seemed to be in droves, spluttering their way towards London. This was not going to be a convoy such as the Atlantic ones. No columns of ships stretching for miles. No zig-zagging and no drastic alterations of course to avoid the U-Boat wolf packs. Air attack and the presence of German motor torpedo craft, known as E-Boats, were the danger now. Our destination was not very far away in sailing terms and in two columns we proceeded on a pre-arranged route which was marked and on steering courses which had been laid down before leaving Southend. Upon arrival off the beaches we were allocated an anchorage which I would have called congested in normal terms, and told to await the arrival alongside of the landing craft into which we were to discharge our cargo. They were working flat out going back and forth to the beaches discharging the cargo and then returning immediately to fill up again. Our discharging gear, winches, derricks, guys etc., were already rigged and the next morning the LCTs came alongside and we started to un-load. The troops had been taken off as soon as we anchored.

It was a slow process with the ship's derricks having to be repositioned frequently in order to plumb directly over the available deck space on the landing craft. Before completion we had one bit of good fortune. One of the landing craft was just about ready to cast off and head for the beaches. There was just enough deck space for one more vehicle. The vehicles were carefully stowed on the LCT in order that they might drive straight down the ramp onto the beach. The space remaining was surrounded by other vehicles and as we were slowly lowering the last one the sling parted and it went hurtling down onto the landing craft. I expected the worst and thought of three or four vehicles being badly damaged. Amazingly, it dropped square on its four wheels right into the open space, bounced a few times but did not touch a thing. The battles were raging on the Continent and our role was to get back to London as quickly as possible to re-load, as more and more equipment and munitions would be needed. After the usual 'make ready for sea routine' the hatches were battened down and the derricks lowered; we set off in company with other vessels who had completed discharging and commenced our return voyage to London.

We were steaming along peacefully and making good progress in calm weather conditions when at some time towards the end of the middle watch, 12 to 4, there was a loud explosion. I was off watch and asleep in my bunk and would have been called at 03.45 to take over the bridge watch at 04.00. I was not quite sure what had happened but was soon dressed and on deck. Such is the training you receive over the years that my first reaction was to assess the damage and to take soundings to see if we were taking in water. With the ship's carpenter in attendance with his sounding rod and both of us carrying torches, we went up the fore-deck on the portside. We got no further than abreast of No. 2 hatch where the deck had been opened up as if by a huge tin opener. Down below could be seen the extent of the hull damage made by the torpedo and it was obvious nothing could be done to prevent the water from pouring into the empty hold. Soundings were of no importance now with the ship filling up. Evacuation drill came next as it was obvious we would have to abandon ship. All crew were accounted for and seen to be wearing their life jackets.

When at sea during the war the ship's lifeboats were always kept swung outward ready for instant lowering. To prevent any damage caused by movement of the ship the boats were bowsed in tightly against a spar stretched between the davits. The spar was fitted with two large soft pads which we called puddings. The boat lay against them when the bowsing-in wires were tightened up by means of bottle screw or other device. A stenhouse slip was also fitted which needed just a tap with a hammer to release the whole apparatus. You can imagine what could have happened in an Atlantic storm if the lifeboats had been left hanging free. Despite these precautions boats were lost at sea in extreme weather conditions.

We were now waiting orders to leave; the wires had been released and the lifeboats lowered to main deck level. The boat's crew stepped in and when the order to abandon came my boat was supposed to be put in the water. I gave the order for this but as the boat descended a few feet it began to tip outward. A wire had become caught on the inboard gunwale. There was no way of releasing it with the weight of the boat and personnel holding it firmly. There was no telling how long the *Samwake* would remain afloat so something had to be done quickly. One crew member in the boat was an engine room greaser. He was a huge man with arms like tree trunks. I sent him back up the boat ladder and into the crew's alleyway to bring the big fire axe which was positioned on the bulkhead. He braced himself, raised the axe above his head and brought it down on the wire with all his power. The wire parted and the boat righted itself, but it wasn't only the wire that felt the blade of the axe. The gunwale had been sliced down for about 4″ and these were steel lifeboats. Had we been fitted with the conventional clinker built wooden lifeboat which I had been used to who knows how far the axe might have gone.

Suddenly a thought struck me and I jumped back on board and found my way up two steel staircases to the officers' accommodation and so into my own cabin. There was a picture of my wife on the bulkhead. It was coloured and quite a good size. You cannot hang pictures on ship's bulkheads whether they be wood or steel. They have to be attached by screws top and bottom to prevent any movement. I had come to retrieve the photograph but had no screwdriver. There was no other way but to smash the glass and drag it out. This I managed and cut my hand in the process. But what to do with it now? I couldn't carry it around like that, so I folded it in four and pushed it inside my uniform jacket. In married life there are many stories of getting into the good books again or having your stripes back. That blood-stained photograph was well received and is still with us after fifty years. There were many other things I could have brought with me but I knew the photograph was the most important.

We were not the only ship to have been attacked but were as far as we knew the only one to be sunk. The official report said that an eastbound convoy heading for the River Thames from the Normandy beaches was attacked in the English Channel by three German E-Boats from the 6th Flotilla. During the battle the *Samwake* (in ballast) was sunk in approximate position 50°40′N 00°-31′E and four other vessels were damaged. Some we could see burning in the distance. After we had abandoned ship we stood a little distance off, both boats together. Dawn had broken and daylight was approaching. The other vessels had by now disappeared eastwards. It was calm and we just sat there surveying the scene. It was then decided that there might be a chance of beaching the vessel on the English coast. The Captain's boat went round to the starboard side and he and the 2nd Engineer boarded. I was attempting with my crew to get along-side on the port side from where we had pulled away. I made the stupid mistake of trying to approach the ladder from the forward end and nearly suffered extinction. As we came nearer to No. 2 hold we were suddenly drawn towards the gaping hole in the hull by the sheer volume of the inrushing water. These were anxious moments and it took some time and much of the crew's strength to fend the boat off and prevent it being drawn into the hole. I had visions of doing trips around No. 2 hold, but they would be one-way trips. I thought later on that since we had been struck on the port side and as I remembered the routing instructions, we would by now be well over on the English side of the Channel, so the E-Boats must have been marauding near our coast. The beaching operation was not feasible so both boats stood off again and watched the *Samwake* getting lower in the water. It took a long time but after approximately four hours she did not break up but just gracefully put her head down and slowly disappeared with her stern and propeller almost vertical at the end. I thought of the new coat of paint I had had applied before leaving Boston; what a waste! But had it been left in the paint locker it would still have hit the bottom.

We were eventually picked up by an armed trawler which seemed to have just come upon us. After we were safely installed on board it was decided that we would tow the two lifeboats astern. They soon broke away and were left behind to ride up and down the English Channel with the tides in control. After the customary mug of tea I went up in the wheelhouse to chat with the skipper. She was quite an old craft and to gain entry into the wheelhouse meant climbing an inside ladder and then pushing back a sort of trap door. The skipper, who was a regular trawler man and in the RNR, told me that he was on his way from Milford Haven to Grimsby and was in Boom Defence operations. He had been on his feet for thirty-six hours with only a young PO to assist in the navigating. He asked if I was familiar with the routing instructions. This, of course, I was after nearly five years of convoy sailing, so I suggested that he go below and have a rest. It was decided that we head for Dover which was on our way and as he was bound for Grimsby re-routing would be necessary. Before arriving off the break-water I had him called so that he could take his vessel into port and alongside the allocated berth. There were ambulances there to meet us but fortunately we had no casualties. All the crew were able to walk ashore and board the coaches which were there to take us to some reception hall. Before leaving the trawler I shook hands with the skipper and thanked him for picking us up. He replied by thanking me for bringing his craft to Dover and allowing him a brief rest. I am sure he would have lots more before having to carry on to Grimsby.

I have the greatest admiration for the WVS – the Women's Voluntary Services – who looked after us during our brief stay in Dover. They were very kind without being patronising and helped us in many ways. An excellent meal was laid on for us in the hall and I will always remember their knowledge of the needs of a surviving mariner for at each seating place there was a large bottle of beer. Arrangements were made for the issue of rail warrants to take us to our homes and there was an advance of pay. But first we had to have a change of clothing or to be kitted out. We were taken to local tailors and I chose a sports jacket and a pair of flannel trousers. Being of standard size and weight I was lucky and did very well. The outfit was worn for years.

To get us on our way home we had first to go to London and we travelled there in a double-decker bus. Old habits and trad-itions die hard, for in the front on the top deck sat the Captain and his officers, further back the POs and the lower ranks down below. It was quite a leisurely journey going through the lovely Kent countryside. There was no M2, M20 or by-passes so it took quite a time. There was no hurry for we had no specific train to catch but would be landed at the appropriate station in the capital. There were stops in the country for calls of nature and at one stage it was decided that a little liquid refreshment would go down very well, and so the driver was asked to look out for a suitable watering hole. We pulled up shortly afterwards at a large establishment surrounded by a car park. Eyes were raised when we all trooped in, officers to the saloon bar, crew to the public, and the proprietor just looked at us. It was not until the orders started coming in that she spoke. No, she could not serve us, not even with one glass each, there was only enough for her regular customers, and no way was she going to part with it. So it was back to the bus and try the next one. The reception here was entirely different. After hearing who and what we were the landlady called a halt to all serving until we had each been given a drink. I say given for we were not even asked to pay. From somewhere she produced some pork pies, cut them up and placed them on the counter. When thanking her I mentioned how we had been treated at our first stop. She asked the name of the place and then said, 'That was shameful. I happen to be the Mayor of this Borough and will certainly bring this matter up at the next Council meeting.'

My departure station in London was Euston where, understandably in the present conditions, I had to wait for a long time before boarding a train bound for the north-west. None of my companions were heading that way so I sat in a crowded carriage for a journey which seemed endless. I had no complaints for I was going home safe and well.

I arrived home next morning in my new outfit with the old gear in a cheap suitcase, plus my sextant which I had in the lifeboat and, still folded in four, the blood-stained photograph.

* * *

I was now on what was officially called 'shipwreck leave'. Normally the balance of wages with deductions would be made up by the Captain or the accountants of the owners or managers of the vessel. This was not possible in this case as I was not officially working for them as my account, which included allowances to my wife, was controlled in London. It was headed 'Liberation of Europe Account of Wages'. They had all my particulars which gave my address as being in the City of Chester. Some intelligent person in the Ministry of War Transport worked out that the nearest seaport to Chester was Connah's Quay on the River Dee in Flintshire, North Wales. I was informed that all my documents stating balance of wages had been sent to the officer-in-charge at the Custom House, Connah's Quay. It was not too far away, about ten miles, and there was a bus service. The gentleman I had come to see was out when I arrived. He was apparently having his lunch break and I was told where I could find him. He was in the saloon bar of what must have been the sub-office, for the name of the inn was the Custom House. After establishing his identity I introduced myself and we chatted for some time over a couple of beers. Later we returned to the 'Main Office' and my papers were produced. There didn't seem much that my new friend could do, as he had never had to deal with a subject like this before, so I suggested that I take the documents with me and go the next morning to the Mercantile Marine Office in Liverpool.

This I did and everything was stamped and sealed satisfactorily. The column in my Discharge Book, which was headed 'Description of Voyage' was marked instead of the usual 'Foreign' with 'Home Trade Operations', whatever that was supposed to mean. I was also issued with some food ration coupons which were absolutely necessary if I was to carry on with my 'shipwreck leave'.

Connah's Quay was a thriving port at the time before the River Dee started to silt up, but this was long before my marine experiences.

It was common practice during the hectic days of the Battle of the Atlantic to have or to make a sizable wallet or pouch to hold important personal documents such as discharge book, Certificate of Competency, identity card etc., and maybe some photographs, a prayer book or rosary. This was attached to a belt which could be strapped to you in the event of the vessel being torpedoed and you having to leave in a hurry. During prolonged attacks it was worn all the time and in quieter times would be lying close to your life jacket and ready to be worn.

I had such a wallet when torpedoed on the *Samwake* but for some reason or other I had unfastened it when in the lifeboat. As described earlier, an attempt was made by the rescuing trawler to tow both lifeboats but this was not successful and they broke adrift.

I was at this time a member of the Navigators and Engineer Officers' Union and after a short time at home I received a letter from the General Secretary returning some of my documents. The text of the letter is as follows:

We enclose herewith wallet and Merchant Navy Officer's Pension Fund Pass Book which have been forwarded to us by a Squadron Leader in the R.A.F. in Newhaven, as having been recovered from the English Channel on the 21st ultimo.

As the Union Membership Book, which was also recovered, was very badly damaged we have pleasure in enclosing herewith a duplicate. You will note that your membership lapsed on the 10th February, 1942 and we trust that you consider bringing it up to date.

We sincerely trust that you suffered no ill effects as the result of the loss of your ship, and should there be any matters on which you seek our advice, please do not hesitate to get in touch with us.

Yours truly,

Despite the solicitous remarks as to my well being I was well and truly reminded that I owed them money. Now, if I hadn't had the Membership Book in the wallet, how long would I have got away with it?

I was most grateful to the Squadron Leader and wrote him a letter of thanks. I presume that the lifeboats were spotted by aircraft who alerted the Air Sea Rescue craft of the RAF who would go out to investigate. Fortunately, it was only my wallet they found and nothing more serious.

Chapter 7

SS *Edward Bruce*

THE 'shipwreck' or 'survivor's leave' as I preferred to call it soon came to an end so I reported back to the Silver Line who had been managers of the *Samwake*. I was instructed to join a vessel called the *Edward Bruce*, at present discharging in Liverpool. This was good news for me for it meant I could travel daily from my home in Chester until the time came to sail. When boarding the vessel I was delighted to find that she was, like the *Samwake*, a Liberty ship, and being familiar with the layout and the navigational and cargo working gear made it easy for me to settle in.

Not all Libertys had the prefix 'Sam'. The *Edward Bruce* was built for the US Maritime Commission in November 1943 by the Bethlehem–Fairfield Shipyard in Baltimore, Maryland. Apart from some slight difference in accommodation layout and the later introduction of Torpedo Net Defence equipment, she was the same solid, efficient and comfortable Liberty that I knew and I was pleased to serve on her as Chief Officer. She was originally launched as the *Samoine* then changed to *Edward Bruce*. I have since learned that the *Edward Bruce* survived the war, was returned to the US Reserve Fleet in 1947 and was scrapped in 1971.

The strength of the Liberty ship was, in my mind, never in doubt. However, I remember one voyage when crossing the Atlantic in extremely bad weather and in ballast with the ship pitching and rolling heavily we found that the corners of the accommodation block amidships, which was one prefabricated section, had lifted at the corners where it was welded to the maindeck. This was really bad weather with extreme pitching and twisting and the propeller thrashing when it lifted out of the water. We were westward bound and one noontime when our position was established we found that we were lying further east than on the previous day.

The convoy was scattered for miles and dispersed. During the worst of the hurricane, for that was what it was, we had two of our lifeboats on the weather side smashed and rendered useless. These were soon replaced when we reached the USA.

Sceptics would say that this all-welded construction was bound to be faulty and that cracks would appear in the hull and ships would be lost. I have always believed that any faults were caused not by the welding but by the welders. It takes some time to train a welder but with this rapid turnout of ships and with some sections being constructed in places far away from the building yard there could have been a lack of training or of inspections. Conventional beams, hatchboards and tarpaulins were the means of battening down the hatches on all of these vessels and on the *Edward Bruce* I saw another glaring mistake by welders. The cleats to hold the battens and wooden wedges securing the tarpaulins should have been fixed with the aperture angled outwards and facing forward on each side and outwards from the centre of each end of the hatch. This was to prevent the wooden wedges being driven out by heavy seas. If angled correctly the wedges would be forced further into the cleat if this was possible but could not be dislodged. The welder fixing the cleats on the coamings of one of the hatches could not have known this for he must have started at one corner of the hatch and carried on placing the cleats all the way around until he came back to his starting point thus having half of them facing the wrong way.

It was now time to get back into the Atlantic and, leaving Liverpool, we took the usual route, picking up other vessels from the Clyde then sailing well north of Ireland. We were bound for New York, and upon arrival there went straight into dry dock. We were not damaged but needed a wash and brush up of the underwater parts. A few other jobs were done, for instance the hatch cleats at No. 2. The dry dock was on the Brooklyn side and near to where I used to dock before the war when trading round the world out via Panama, back via Suez as told in my volume *Seafaring in the Thirties*. I knew this part well. It had been my home port for a few years so I was able to re-visit old haunts and friends. Contact was made again with the English Speaking Union and they delivered on board a large cardboard box full of beautifully knitted woollen garments to keep us warm during the Atlantic winter. There were scarves, mitts, balaclavas and rolled-neck jerseys. The English ladies and their friends must certainly have put a great deal of effort and time into providing us and other vessels with such comforts, but I wondered why it was assumed that all British seamen are six feet or more tall. I stood at five feet six inches.

When loading commenced it was as before: tanks, trucks, ammunition, etc., anything and everything required by the troops on the ground. We expected that we would follow the old pattern up to Bedford Basin, Halifax, Nova Scotia and then eastwards across the Atlantic to the UK, perhaps even back to the Normandy beaches. This was not to be, for our role now was to feed the Allied forces in the Mediterranean directly from the USA.

On one voyage to Naples it must have been a strange sight from ashore to see thirty ships, all Libertys, sailing in single file through the northern end of the Straits of Messina. It seemed as if there were hundreds of small boats, some powered but mostly rowing boats, lining our route and getting as close to the vessels as safety would allow. They were not there to greet us but to beg. Anything that could be thrown, cigarettes, coffee, tea, and so on was gratefully received. It is a wonder some of the craft were not run down, for the nearer they got to the ship the better chance they had of something landing in the boat. I don't recall any tragedies, but there must have been some near misses for we would be steaming at about 10 knots.

When loading in the USA most of the tanks and vehicles were lifted on board by shore cranes. At the discharging ports conditions could be very different. Many ports had been badly damaged by Allied air attack and the discharge of cargo was often done with the ship at anchor using its own equipment to discharge into barges.

Despite there being a war on, ships' derricks, wires and blocks had to be kept in good order and had to conform to Department of Trade or Ministry regulations. All derricks were marked with the number of tons which they could safely lift such as 'SWL 5 tons'. Purchasing wires, runners, etc., all had to be of appropriate size and strength. The equipment was periodically examined to conform with regulations and a certificate issued.

On another voyage to Naples we were fortunate to be allocated a quayside berth but it still meant using our own discharging gear. There were some heavy trucks on deck alongside No. 1 hatch. As I remember it the SWL of No. 1 derricks was 7 tons. The heavy lift derricks were at No. 2 and No. 4.

One morning I saw that the trucks were about to be put ashore. An American major was on board and he was anxious to take delivery. I could see that the weight to be lifted was far in excess of 7 tons. It wasn't just the trucks but what was in them. Each one was completely filled with guns, stores and other requirements for his unit. I was in a quandary. What to do if the derrick bent? I pointed out to the major that the derricks could only safely lift 7 tons and there could be an accident. He seemed quite unconcerned and said, 'If the derrick breaks we will give you another one,' and he meant it for on the quay were a number of derricks constructed for Liberty ships and brought over for any such emergency. The Americans certainly thought of everything.

On the return journey to the USA we would, in the winter months, call at Casablanca and load a small quantity of phosphates as ballast to make our westward passage more comfortable. This was discharged in Norfolk, Virginia and both Norfolk, Va. and Newport News, Va. became our loading ports.

These Atlantic convoys were made up mostly by American vessels and on one particular voyage we were the only British ship in the company of forty or fifty American vessels, all of us Liberty ships. We had the doubtful honour of being appointed Rear Commodore. This meant that our station in the convoy was at the rear of the centre column. It was our task to see that other vessels in the rear received the flag or Aldis lamp signals from the Commodore and acted upon them. It was a doubtful honour, for we were ill-equipped for this sort of duty, and it meant a lot of extra work without an increase in manpower. All American ships carried larger crews and had signallers properly trained in morse lamp signalling, whereas our normal bridge watch at sea consisted of the officer of the watch, the man at the wheel and an apprentice. At times there was enough to do to maintain our station. Often I would ask for the help of one of the Radio Officers if the signalling by the lamp was a little too rapid. I suppose to be chosen was something.

We did later on receive a sort of backhanded compliment. We were bound for Norfolk, Va. and at a predetermined position some distance off the coast about abeam of Chesapeake Bay we were to alter course and run into the Bay. One morning at dawn I was able to determine our position by star observation. It was a clear morning and my sextant sights were good. The position I had arrived at showed, when marked on the chart, that we were some miles past the area in which we should have altered course. I was so confident of the accuracy of my sights that I called up the Commodore and signalled my findings. About ten minutes later a flag hoist went up to all ships indicating that there would be an emergency alteration to port. When all ships had acknowledged the signal the new course was hoisted and we headed towards the coast. Maybe other vessels had taken star sights but I felt that I had triggered it off.

I had formed the impression that some of the American vessels did not have too many experienced personnel on board. This was not surprising when you consider that their Merchant Marine must have nearly doubled since they entered the war. In a Norfolk newspaper it was reported with great pride the story of one Master who was only twenty-one. Following the leader and obeying instructions was apparently easy but I wondered how they would cope if still there and operating in the commercial world. Liberty ships were being launched by the day and these young men were essential. The American Merchant Marine suffered heavy casualties and operated in all spheres of the conflict.

* * *

Most males could be accused of doing silly things in their time just for the fun of it, and none were more susceptible to this than the seamen. Maybe this trend was developed on long voyages through loneliness. One example of this was when we were discharging in Taranto and lying at anchor. There hadn't been much chance of a break ashore for some time. Four of us engaged an Italian boatman to row us ashore and be on hand to bring us back. There was not much to do but the local wine went down very well. When the time came for us to return, the four of us, Chief Officer, 2nd Officer, 1st Radio Officer and 2nd Radio Officer, were all, shall we say, a little jolly. We had enjoyed the break and were happy. About halfway between the quay and the ship the 1st Radio Officer fell overboard. We were in uniform and his cap was floating on the surface of the water. This looked like a serious situation until his head appeared and he said, 'It's lovely in here. Why don't you come in?' Whereupon we tipped ourselves out of the boat and swam around. The boatman was panic stricken. What if he had lost us? After a while we climbed back into the boat with the help of the boatman. It is easy to get into the water from a rowing boat but most difficult to get back in again, especially if clothed. Even a lifeboat is hard to board from the water. Fortunately it was dark and we managed to get to our respective cabins without much fuss.

After loading about 2,000 tons of phosphates as ballast in Casablanca we were lying at a layby berth waiting for other vessels to complete loading and join us in forming a convoy. We were all battened down and ready for sea. Two or three of us were standing on deck idling the time away until departure. A drink was suggested but we had nothing on board at all and hadn't had for some time. We were dressed in 'whites', no jacket but a shirt with epaulettes. The 2nd Mate had a great idea. Pulling off his shirt and removing the epaulettes he threw it to an Arab lad on the quay and told him to buy something to drink. After a while the boy came back with a small bottle of what could be described as 'hootch'. Taken with a liberal quantity of orange squash it was barely palatable. We managed a couple each and the bottle was then placed on the deck in my wardrobe. Decks in cabins and alleyways were of composition covering the steel and then painted with red deck paint. We sailed in the early evening but ran into a heavy swell as we moved further away from the African coast. When I came off watch at 8 o'clock the following morning and entered my cabin, I could hear a 'chink chink' noise coming from the wardrobe. Afterwards, when the wardrobe door was opened, all that could be seen on the deck was broken glass lying on badly blistered red deck paint which looked as if it had been coated with paint remover. My early days at sea before the war serving on hard case tramp ships proved to be an asset for the 'no star' cuisine served up with Board of Trade rations: salt pork, salt beef and hard biscuits, must have accustomed my stomach to accept almost anything with no ill effect. A protective lining maybe!

The carriage of war supplies across the Atlantic continued except for one voyage when we loaded a full cargo of coal at Newport News for a North African port. It would be on this crossing that one night there was an explosion and two vessels to the far right of the convoy were ablaze. It meant immediate action stations. We later learned that it was not an enemy attack but that two vessels, one a Liberty and one a tanker, had been in collision and had gone up in flames. The convoy as always obeyed the rules and steamed on. I have no idea of the outcome or number of lives lost.

The method of loading the coal was an eye-opener to me. I had loaded coal in the UK and Continent and the usual way of loading was for a wagon to be raised, the pins knocked out of one end and then the wagon tipped to empty its load into whichever hatch was directly underneath. This meant endless shifting of ship to distribute the coal, and later the employment of trimmers to shovel the coal into the ends and wings of the cargo hold not directly under the drop. In Newport News they were far more efficient. Rail lines led to a large hopper into which the coal from wagons carrying 40 tons was dumped. This was high above the ship and below the hopper or bin was a huge protruding arm, 6–8 feet wide, which could extend to any distance required. The end was opened and closed by jaws. This whole contraption was moved along the loading berth to any position required and high above any obstacles of derricks etc. on board. It was controlled by one man in his cabin overlooking the ship. When the arm was lowered into the ship's hold the jaws were opened and it spewed its constant supply of coal in any direction required to fill the spaces. There was no need to move the ship along the quay, the loading arm was moved to wherever required. Trimming was not necessary as the arm or chute could protrude into all corners of the cargo hold. It was also very fast. We were not long alongside before we were battening down and ready for sea. Twenty years later the old system was still used in most of the ports in the UK.

* * *

We had our Motor Torpedo Boats, the Germans had their E-Boats and the Americans had their version, which were larger and I believe faster.

We loaded four of these craft in Norfolk, Va. to be discharged in Naples. They were, of course, deck cargo and before they could be loaded a steel trellis platform was welded to the deck on each side of No. 2 and No. 4 hatches. This was where the ship's heavy lift derricks of 50 tons and 30 tons were situated, which would be needed for discharging in Naples, which we knew would be whilst the vessel was lying at anchor. The craft, seated in heavy wooden cradles, were lifted on board by shore cranes and then securely lashed with wires and bottle screws to the steel platform. The voyage across the Atlantic was in convoy with American escorts. The U-Boat war was not yet over but most sinkings occurred nearer the coasts and sailing in mid-Atlantic was uneventful.

Upon arrival in Naples we duly went to an anchorage and commenced discharging our normal cargo into lighters which were very soon alongside. When the time came for these very modern craft to be discharged we were visited by four young men who each was to take command. We had assumed that we had brought them for the American Forces, as they had been loaded in America and escorted by the American Navy, but no, these young men were British RNVR officers who had been in this area for some time, and had seen quite a lot of action. The Captain invited them to his cabin for a drink and together we heard of some of their exploits. I could just see them racing in and out of the Messina Straits firing their deck mounted guns at everything in sight. They were brave young men, all volunteers, similar in a way to the Spitfire pilots. The acceptance party went on for quite some time until the craft were safely in the water, then the young lieutenants returned to their base leaving their new commands to be towed round and removed from the wooden cradles.

Before leaving, one of the four invited me to go out with him on trials and said he would come back when he had filled up with fuel. This happened a couple of days later when he came alongside one of the barges into which we were discharging. It was a marvellous experience for me. After passing through the breakwater he opened up the throttle, or put the handle down, and we shot forward at speeds I could never have imagined in water. This was different from 7- or 8-knot convoys and it was exhilarating to be doing 40 knots or more. When returning my new friend decided to show me how they did things. He gave an order and four ratings lined up forward in their white rolled-neck jerseys just as would happen on a submarine. When near to the barge on which I was to be landed he gave the order, 'Heaving line away.' The rating entrusted to this task did just that but instead of holding onto one end of it so as to pass a mooring rope ashore, he threw the lot. We now had to take a round turn and come in again. This time it was successful and I wished them luck as I left and climbed the pilot ladder to my own craft. Who knows who they would be blasting in a day or two. They were all volunteers but obviously not professional seamen.

* * *

Just one more part cargo of phosphate from Casablanca to Norfolk, Va. and then down to Cuba to load sugar. This was good news for all on board for we learned that we were to load a full cargo in the port of Nuevitas and our destination was the UK. Load Line Regulations, like any other rules imposed by the Board of Trade or the Ministry of Transport, were strictly adhered to. This I have mentioned before. We were loading in what was called a Summer Zone which would allow the vessel to be loaded down to her summer marks with the allowed freeboard. The rules also state that whichever zone you subsequently sail into, the freeboard assigned to that zone must be complied with. As we would have to enter a Winter Zone, which would mean having a bigger freeboard, calculations would have to be made to take into account the consumption of fuel and fresh water. Then one morning we received a message brought on board by a member of the British Consulate giving us permission to load to tropical marks. This meant that we could carry about an extra 400 tons. This was indeed an added bonus but I remember roughly working out how many weekly rations of sugar each person in the UK would receive or how long our cargo of sugar would last. It wasn't very long at all.

After completion we sailed for New York to join an eastbound convoy. Some of us were more than delighted when in the final orders we were listed as being bound for Liverpool. It was now the end of March 1945. This was a large convoy which included escort oilers, and, despite a period of bad weather when the convoy became scattered, we made good progress. In fact, I think it was about the shortest crossing I had made throughout the war. Our station was near to the Commodore ship and the senior escort vessel. One morning during the 4 a.m.–8 a.m. watch I intercepted a message between these vessels which was confirmed by the Radio Officer on watch, and was of great significance. It was 12 April 1945 and President Roosevelt had died. I had the greatest admiration for him and remembered how he had induced or persuaded his Government and the American people to supply us with military equipment, arms, ammunition and food. The American Navy even escorted convoys part of the way across the Atlantic and this was well before Pearl Harbour and the Americans' entry into the war. My feelings were such that I already had the Red Ensign flying at half mast before a general signal was sent out.

The Atlantic was now a different ocean. In March there were twelve ships sunk and in April only nine. In peace time, nine ships sunk in a month would have been a disaster but this was a small figure compared to the 120 ships in December 1941. About a week before arriving in Liverpool two ships in this convoy were torpedoed and sunk. One was a British tanker, the other an American Liberty ship. The U-boats were now suffering very heavy losses, especially in the approaches to Britain and France. Many were surrendering. Official figures show that more than 600 U-Boats were destroyed during the conflict.

After completion of discharge in Liverpool we again set off to cross the North Atlantic. It was the usual pattern. When your scheduled time of sailing came you cast off, proceeded to the locks and were lowered into the River Mersey, then went out to Liverpool Bay to form up with other vessels making up this particular convoy which was to be the last one that I would sail in.

* * *

We sailed with almost a new crew. Most of the officers who had joined with me from the *Samwake* after she was torpedoed left to have some leave and then find other berths. The crew members, having completed their obligation by the Terms of Articles of Agreement, were entitled to sign off and they did. I was lucky; this was my home port. I lived just twenty miles away and was able to spend each night at home.

The war in Europe was almost over, the U-Boats had taken a terrible battering but there was still the danger of some marauding submarine anxious to make a final killing, so we still had an escort, one of which was a merchant aircraft carrier. This was a larger merchant vessel which had been converted by constructing a flight deck above the main and accommodation decks.

After a few days at sea we heard that the war in Europe had ended on 9 May 1945. The German High Command had surrendered to Field Marshal Montgomery. The Atlantic Battle was now over and we were let loose to make our way as we pleased towards our destination. Most of us were bound in the same direction, at least towards the American continent, so we had company for a few days until we fanned out and set course for our respective destinations.

Shortly after we left Liverpool a stowaway was discovered on board. It was a feathered one, a pigeon, not seeking to go anywhere but just looking for a place to land and rest. It was absolutely exhausted but soon bucked up when the crew took over the role of nursemaid. The carpenter made a roost with perch, and all kinds of delicacies were offered like milk, water, corn and greens. It was not uncommon for migrating birds to land exhausted on ships but they soon recovered and took off again in an attempt to catch up with the main flight. Our feathered friend showed no signs of leaving. Life on board was too comfortable and whether it was planned or not emigration to Canada was now the only option. As we progressed further into the Atlantic, a point of no return was reached and our friend remained with us.

We were bound for Montreal to load a full cargo of grain. Our destination after loading was not confirmed until we were almost down to our marks. Grain cargoes from Canada were usually bulk cargoes but this time the grain was in bags. We had hoped for a quick return eastwards across the Atlantic but this seemed hardly likely with bagged grain. When the final orders came we learned that we were bound for Greece. The Greeks had had a hard time under the Nazi occupation and were now crying out for food supplies, so despite our disappointment at not returning to the UK we realised that this was to be a humanitarian voyage and was gladly accepted. At any grain terminal or loading berth vast numbers of pigeons collect and take up residence, as there is always plenty of food. Our addition to the flock or flight seemed to be accepted and some of the crew claimed to have seen him or her flying around and, at times, doing a sortie over the *Edward Bruce*. To me pigeons all look alike but it may have been saying thank you and goodbye.

Before reaching Canada we had perhaps our final Atlantic hazard. We ran into pack ice which had drifted south. Visibility was very poor at the time and some ships suffered minor damage but we managed to avoid striking the ice by posting treble lookouts and making many alterations of course and speed.

Steaming down the St. Lawrence after leaving Montreal and just after passing Quebec, I noticed half-a-dozen destroyers and corvettes, Canadian and British, lying two abreast on the opposite side of the river. They had done a magnificent job of providing us with protection against U-Boats. Now they had no job to do so no doubt were well pleased about that. I felt a little sad. It is hard to explain but after years of accepting the danger and the prospect of being torpedoed when there could be a strange feeling of elation with the adrenalin flowing, now all these feelings would disappear.

I had sailed independently during the war, as recorded earlier, but always we set out in convoy and were later dispersed to carry on alone to our predetermined destination. Crossing the Atlantic, particularly if westward bound and light ship in winter gales with the ship pitching and rolling almost to the extreme and the constant threat of U-Boat attack was, to say the least, most uncomfortable. All this was forgotten after arriving in the US or Canadian port where the bars were open until late at night, the lights were on, no blackout and there was plenty of food with no rationing. There was also the gratification of having had a successful trip and the knowledge that your prayers had been answered. Your batteries would be re-charged before making the return voyage and once again the adrenalin would flow. These feelings were now about to change.

The killing, the tortures, the hardships had ended in this sphere of the globe and countless thousands were overjoyed and proud of the victories achieved. How then could I feel sad? Some strange reaction, I suppose. Passing the destroyers, I was prompted to call them up by Aldis lamp signal and my message read, 'Sorry you are not coming with us.' The next morning we were well out at sea and heading for the Straits of Gibraltar then into the Mediterranean and eastwards to Piraeus, the port of Athens.

Upon arrival in Piraeus we were ordered to anchor in the harbour and the next morning commenced discharging with the ship's equipment into barges. The barges were dumb barges (no power) and were brought out by small tugs. It was now obvious why we had loaded a bagged cargo. This was the only way that grain could be discharged in this port and it could be easily distributed to other parts of the country. There was one upsetting aspect of this discharge. The barge operators were apparently paid according to the number of bags landed on the quayside. They were in a great hurry, scurrying to and fro and inevitably some bags were torn and the loose grain lay on the bottom of the barge. They were only small craft and after many trips quite a considerable quantity of loose grain would remain on board. This meant that in order to keep the craft stable a smaller number of bags would be loaded, so to get the maximum payment the loose grain was shovelled overboard on the outward trip. Before we sailed I noted that none of the bags had been moved from the quay. This grain was a gift but I didn't see much sign of gratitude. Part of the cargo was to be discharged in Volos on the east side of the mainland. We were soon there and again discharged whilst at anchor.

* * *

The German war machine had collapsed and victory in Europe was established. In the Far East Japan was on the verge of collapse yet there was still fighting here in Greece. A communist takeover of the country was being resisted by the Greek Government and army and they were backed up by British troops. Whilst in Volos the Captain and myself were invited to avail ourselves of the facilities offered by the British Army officers' mess which was near the quayside. It was a medical officers' mess, the only one, and used by doctors, medics, nurses and combat officers having a short break from the fighting. There were also the Army padres and one, a most remarkable man, was a Catholic priest who stood about 6' 4". He was the confidant of all ranks in the area regardless of their denomination. He could also hold his own at the bar, never wore a 'dog collar' and was usually dressed in khaki shirt and shorts. One evening a couple of infantry officers down from the line were enjoying a well earned rest and the comforts of the officers' mess bar. They were impeccably dressed in their No. 1 uniforms and looked very smart. As the evening wore on and their glasses were filled and re-filled they became a little boisterous and when introduced to the padre made some snide remarks about how he was the first man of the cloth they had seen dressed like that and without his badge of office, the 'dog collar'. The priest stood this for a while but then came over to them and, to the surprise of the other occupants, instead of quietly remonstrating said, 'If you two would like to come outside and try and put one on me you are welcome to do so.' For all his outward bluntness he performed his pastoral duties with sincerity and piety and was respected by all who knew him, and his advice was well received.

One morning when he was visiting the ship I told him of some disquiet among some members of the crew. Perhaps they were expecting to return to the UK but this was not to be. He suggested that he went aft to the crew's quarters and talked to them. It was during the mid-morning break and he stayed with them until they were due to resume their duties. Whether he preached damnation, counselled them or threatened them I will never know but they were very subdued after his visit.

* * *

Our next voyage ended in Bizerta, Tunisia. It had been a long war and perhaps this was having some effect on me for I felt very jaded and worn out, so I decided that I would seek medical advice ashore. We had received orders that we were to go next to Bona, Algeria and load a cargo of phosphate for Fremantle, Australia. This was not what was expected for the main topic of conversation at this time was where and what cargo we would load for our homeward run. There were certainly some glum faces on board but orders are orders and we had all signed on for a two-year period before we left Liverpool. All foreign going voyages were agreed to be of two years' duration but the agreement was cancelled if in the meantime you returned to the UK. It was going to be hard to write home and say that we were heading the other way.

Keeping my appointment ashore I had the usual blood pressure, pulse and heart beat tests and then was invited to strip to the waist and lie on the couch. Then came the tap tap tapping on my torso and a worried look appeared on the doctor's face. I was advised to leave the ship and come ashore into hospital as I had an enlarged liver which was very serious. I could not do this. I felt I must complete the voyage and found it hard to accept the findings. I was then told that if I intended to sail to Australia then I must keep to a strict diet which he would prepare for me. No this, no that, and certainly no alcohol and only bottled water, crates of which were put on board. My biggest worry was whether I should write and tell my wife. I decided, I think wisely, against this as I really didn't feel that ill and was carrying on as usual. Would I make it to Fremantle, or should I have gone ashore in Bizerta?

It didn't take long to load in Bona and we were soon on our way eastward and through the Suez Canal into the Red Sea and then made passage across the Indian Ocean to western Australia. I stuck strictly to the diet or as closely to it as ship-board cuisine would allow. The whole voyage from Bona with delays in the Canal transit could take us over a month, so I had plenty of time to reflect or worry.

At this time Australia had very strict rules regarding livestock, and no animals or birds from foreign parts were allowed into the country. Therefore we had to lie at anchor outside the harbour until we had been inspected by the appropriate authority. A few of the crew had picked up canaries, probably in Suez, which they hoped to take home. There was also a pet monkey which didn't belong to anyone in particular. The canaries had to be destroyed there and then preferably by the owners, but the monkey presented quite a problem. We would not be allowed to enter harbour with it on board and neither would anyone take it away. It also had to be killed. I was press-ganged into taking on the role of executioner as I had been issued when I first joined the ship with a .38 revolver. It was a most distasteful job and as I approached him sitting on a bollard he looked at me, no doubt wondering what that strange thing was that I was pointing. For a long time afterwards I could see him looking at me with those completely innocent eyes.

Shortly after the commencement of this voyage the war in the

Pacific ended with the Japanese officially surrendering to the Allies on 2 September 1945. It was now all over and we on the *Edward Bruce* would have no further role and could only revert to the carriage of commercial cargoes and peaceful voyages. We would certainly load a cargo in these parts for home.

We entered the harbour the following morning and were securely moored about 8 a.m. Fremantle is an open harbour and it was probably low water, for the maindeck bulwarks were just about level with the quay. The stevedores were already there and waiting to board and commence discharging. Unions were even at this time at the end of the war becoming strong and influential. Although we were lying close alongside and level with the quay they refused to come on board until a proper substantial ship's gangway had been rigged and placed in position. This took a little time and was always put into use after the ship had been seen to be securely moored. When the gangway was in place with man ropes, stanchions and even a lifebuoy at the shipboard end, the stevedores came on board by just stepping onto the bulwark and onto the maindeck both for'd and aft. Never mind the gangway, that didn't seem important any more.

When the discharging was fully under way I had to pay attention to my illness and the diet. Arrangements had been made through the ship's Agents for me to be taken to the local hospital for examination and checks. I explained all that had happened and was given a real going over. The doctor then seemed a little puzzled as to why I was there. I told him the whole story and of my miserable voyage across the Indian Ocean. He looked straight at me and said, 'There is absolutely nothing wrong with you and all systems are in good working order, so don't worry any more.' After thanking him profusely

I hurried out of the hospital and headed for the nearest bar. After a while I ordered a taxi and returned on board. This was our first day in Fremantle and after being pronounced fit I really felt fit and ready to enjoy the rest of the day.

Unfortunately this was not to be for before the day ended a terrible tragedy occurred on board. The Licensing Laws at this time in Australia appertaining to the sale of alcoholic drinks were quite archaic, with limited opening hours and a closure time of 6 p.m. This led to the stupid and disgusting habit of some males drinking as much as possible in the limited time allowed. In some bars there was a 'beat the record' contest just before the closing hour. The test was to see who could drink or 'down' a schooner of beer in the shortest time. Some would make themselves sick in attempting to establish a new time. Deck watches had been suspended and the crew were given shore leave in the afternoon. They had not had a break for a long time, nor had they had any drink. Those who frequented the bars would soon be aware of the drinking laws and perhaps tried to ape the Australians and their stupid end of time act.

I am not sure how or why it happened but it transpired that one of the able seamen and one of the ordinary seamen had had a fierce argument ashore and this became more heated when they returned on board. It may have had something to do with families in Liverpool from where the crew came. It ended tragically with the able seaman taking his sheath knife and fatally stabbing the ordinary seaman. An RN Submarine Depot ship was lying further along the quay; a request for help brought the surgeon on board and he immediately called an ambulance. It was too late, however, for the ordinary seaman died before reaching hospital. It was quite normal for seamen to have a knife. When working on deck it was worn in a sheath on a belt and was at hand if needed to cut rope or twine. The Bosun not only had a sheath knife but also a small marlin spike which was a sort of badge of office.

I did not witness any of the above having returned on board after the ambulance had left. The duty deck officer, keeping the 'night on board' told me all he knew and that the Captain was ashore with the Harbour Authorities. In Liberty ships the whole of the accommodation was in one block amidships, with the crew being on the lower deck. On inquiring if anyone knew where the AB was I learned that he was still on board but in hiding. The 3rd Mate, the duty officer, was sent ashore to call the local police and some of the crew were posted by the gangway with suitable means of protection to prevent the AB getting ashore. I then decided to look for him and as a precaution took my .38 revolver with me. First I did the after deck and steering flat, calling his name frequently. Then the fore deck. All was very quiet but there was still no sign of him. These ships had the standard lookout or 'crow's nest' on the foremast. It was never used in my time, for extra lookouts were always posted in the many gun emplacements on board. However, he may have gone up there and I was tempted to climb the ladder but what if he leaned over the nest and struck me with the knife? I soon abandoned that idea and it was whilst wondering what to do next that I saw a couple of feet sticking out from underneath one of the cargo winch bedding frames. I called his name and kicked his feet. With that he wormed his way out and stood up. I asked him to come with me. He was very respectful, quite subdued and in shock. There was no need even to show the gun. He walked quietly and slowly to my cabin where two detectives were waiting. He was then taken into custody and I was sad to see him led away for he had a record of good behaviour and was a good seaman.

It was not a very quick discharge, the cargo having to be grabbed out and then loaded into trucks to be taken away to various warehouses. Even after completion we were not allowed to leave the port until the police had completed their inquiries.

A couple of days after the murder I went with the Captain to the prison where the accused was being held in order to sign him off or terminate the agreement signed in Liverpool at the commencement of the voyage, to pay him the balance of wages due and also hand over his personal possessions. We sat in the Governor's office and he was brought in. The change in him was remarkable. He seemed to have aged and was ashen faced. He duly signed his release and counted the money due which the Governor took charge of, then was led away. It was the last time I would see him and I felt sad to think that what should have been a relaxing time ashore should end like this. A few days afterwards the funeral took place of the victim. He was buried in the local cemetery with all dignity. The Captain and myself attended on behalf of the ship and the police and Harbour Authorities were represented. Before leaving the cemetery a very moving incident occurred. A woman who was there tending some other grave came to us and said, 'Please inform the relatives of this poor lad that I have the same name as him and as long as I live I will look after the grave.'

We were detained in port for quite a while and three members of the crew had to remain as witnesses. I was also subpoenaed to appear as a witness for the defence. I believe this was because as the Chief Officer I had actually employed the defendant and though the Bosun was the person responsible for his duties it would then be assumed that I would be able to testify as to his character.

With the war being now over and surrenders being completed we would be needed to supply raw materials and food for the home front and our next destination would surely be the UK. I was not then prepared to stay in Fremantle. A trial had not yet been fixed and telegrams were being passed between solicitors in Liverpool and Fremantle in an attempt perhaps to prove some instability in the mind of the accused. During this time I became quite friendly with one of the detectives who had made the arrest and had visited his home. I soon found out that the archaic licensing laws did not apply to him or his companions. I saw no reason to protest and enjoyed a few good nights out. When the time came for us to depart quite a number of local people were on the quayside to wave us off and wish us well and as could be expected they were predominantly female.

We were able to replenish our deck stores before leaving and had a generous supply of paint which I looked forward to having slapped around to bring the *Edward Bruce* up to the standard which was expected of a well run British merchant ship. All this was to be done on the voyage home and it was home that we were heading for.

* * *

This narrative was to be about how I saw the war at sea through my own experiences when sailing on eight different vessels. The war was now well over but I feel I must complete this voyage. First we had to go to a small port in the Spencer Gulf, South Australia called Port Pirie to load a type of ore. Port Pirie reminded me of western films with the railroad running through the town. I thought the method of loading was a little unusual and certainly of the past. The ore was brought to the ship's side in a large steel tub on a special type of cart drawn by a horse. The tub was then winched on board with the ship's gear tripped and spilled into the hold. There was a constant stream of horses and tubs passing beneath the ship's derricks like an endless belt.

The Spencer gulf brought to mind the grain trade of the square riggers of the twenties and earlier who loaded grain in the Gulf for Europe. It would not take us too long to reach the UK through the Suez Canal but those beautiful ships could be at sea for four months. One of my brothers served as a seaman on the last square rigger under the Red Ensign. It was the four-masted barque *Garthpool* and she took 120 days on passage from Wallaroo just south of Port Pirie to Cobh, or Queenstown as it was called then, for orders. It was Queenstown or Falmouth for orders for these ships, with the cargo possibly having been sold and resold during the passage. The *Garthpool* was wrecked on the Cape Verde Islands 1929–30 with my brother on board.

Having completed loading the iron ore we still had two more ports to visit and were soon on our way to New Zealand to load bales of wool. The first port was Timaru and then down to Bluff both in the South Island. We were well received in both of these ports and I remember when in Bluff and the nearby town of Invercargill noticing that there was a hint of Yorkshire accent in the local speech. I was told that this was because the wool appraisers at one time came out each season from Yorkshire and many, no doubt, settled in the area.

Our final destination was to be Swansea, South Wales, but we had roughly 12,000 miles to steam before ending this voyage. It seemed as if we had been away a long time but it was only nine months. I had made much longer voyages, especially before the war, but the war was over and we had not been able to take part in the victory celebrations, and were anxious to see firsthand what the peace proposals entailed and what was to be the rebuilding programme.

The voyage home was just an ordinary long passage with painting ship and other maintenance work going ahead as planned. At the beginning of this narrative when on the *Voco* I told of how all brasswork and brightwork was painted over with the regulation Admiralty grey paint. This was to prevent any reflection in bright sunlight being observed through a submarine periscope. I could understand the logic when applied to any outside engine-room telegraphs, the whistle on the funnel and the regulation ship's 12″ bell on the fo'c'slehead, but not in relation to the brass in the wheelhouse, especially on the *Edward Bruce* with such small windows. So it was that paint removal from all brass became an important task if the ship was to look well cared for and well run when we arrived at our final port. We had four apprentice deck officers on board serving their four years' Indenture and as budding officers I was sure they would enjoy this job of restoration and so it became their responsibility. It took some time to remove the paint which had been on since building and was 'ship side' or hull paint which was supposed to stay on. Even after the paint had been removed the metal had to be polished and polished many times to bring it up to standard. We fortunately had plenty of the canned liquid polish which came on board with our deck stores in Fremantle. To complete the job I had the four young men start work at 6 a.m. in my watch so that I could supervise the finish. I had

had a lot of experience in brass cleaning in my own apprentice-ship days. After many more rubbings with old bunting (flag material) dipped in the liquid polish it all seemed worthwhile for it was gleaming and was surely testimony to how proud we were of our image of being a smartly run vessel.

A few days later came the anticlimax. I said to one of the apprentices who was on watch with me in the evening 4 to 8, 'What do you think of it now, doesn't it look good?' He replied, 'No, Sir, I liked it better the way it was.' I wasn't too fond of polishing brass myself when I was his age but from now on it was going to be that way. The rest of the voyage went quite smoothly and soon we were all beginning to get the 'Channels'. This is a term used at sea to express the feelings of joy, excite-ment or whatever when coming to the end of a long voyage. We berthed in Swansea on 25 February 1946 and on the 26th the Articles of Agreement were closed and all members of the crew who wished to leave were able to do so. Those who intended to sail again on the vessel would put their signatures to a new Agreement before the commencement of the next voyage. We in the Merchant Navy were not conscripted so did not have to be demobilised. I remained on board for about a week until formally relieved by the next appointed Chief Officer. My wife had come down from Chester to meet me and had been staying in a hotel in Swansea for a couple of days before our arrival. The time came for me to say goodbye to those who had stayed on board and this ended my war-time sailing. But not my sea-going days for this was my career and I remained sailing until 1965 when I was promoted to Marine Superintendent after years in command.

Chapter 8

In Convoy

FROM the outbreak of war the convoy system was put into practice whereby merchant ships were gathered together and sailed in formation protected by naval escorts. This had proved successful towards the end of the Great War of 1914–18. At first there was limited protection as the escorts could only go so far into the Atlantic because of re-fuelling problems. Fleet oilers were not operating and after a certain distance they would have to return to base. At this time almost all the U-Boat activity was concentrated around the approaches to Britain and as the American continent was neutral their waters were free of attack. By the end of July 1942 the pattern had changed and there were more sinkings on the western side of the Atlantic than on the eastern side. After a few days on the westward passage it was then a case of 'We cannot come any further' and ships were left to continue the rest of the voyage unescorted. Some vessels of great speed would sail independently. Coastal command aircraft also had a limited range.

Denmark had fallen to the Germans in April 1940 but it was not until October of that year that we occupied Iceland which had close connections with Denmark.

When in Iceland in the mid-eighties I was told a remarkable

story of how this occupation took place. One morning the inhabitants of Reykjavik woke to see the harbour full of British naval craft both large and small with accompanying assault craft. A party with Marines in attendance landed at the main quayside. First ashore was a gentleman dressed in morning suit and wearing a top hat and carrying a briefcase. He walked into the main square and when met by the leaders of the Government announced that he had come to take over their country. Verbal protests were made and the world informed by radio of this violation whilst at the same time a welcome hand was extended. Not a shot was fired. We had taken it before the Germans and that was vital for the protection of our supply lines. This gentleman who had announced the takeover was the ex-British Ambassador to Denmark who had escaped before it was overrun by the German forces. The island was garrisoned by British troops and later fuel storage tanks were built in one of the nearby fjords, which made it possible for the escorts to re-fuel and so protect the convoy during the whole of the passage. I cannot vouch for the validity of this account of the occupation of Iceland, but would very much like to believe it. In 1944 Iceland became a Republic. I believe this was a fitting reward for their acceptance of the Allied occupation.

The main convoy assembly ports were Liverpool Bay, Milford Haven, Loch Ewe in the north of Scotland, off Southend in the Thames Estuary and off Methil in the Firth of Forth. On the western side of the Atlantic, New York and Halifax, Nova Scotia handled almost all of the eastward runs. Convoys could consist of thirty vessels or up to sixty with ten columns.

Before a convoy sailed, a conference was held ashore attended by the Captains of all ships involved with the Commodore and

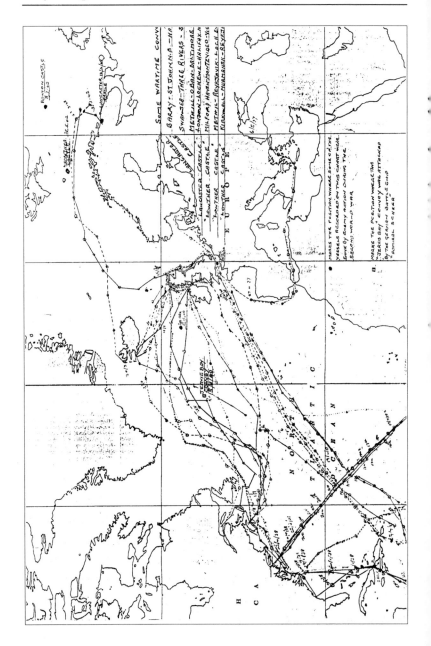

Senior Escort Officer. Instructions were given as to routes, formation, rendezvous and dispersal. Questions were asked and answered. To us on board, especially the navigators, we eagerly awaited being given the information sheet which was laid out on the chartroom table. It gave the names of all ships taking part and their positions in the convoy. It also named the destination of each vessel. This was at times not as informative as it may seem for on many occasions you were listed as bound for Loch Ewe in north-west Scotland where you would be given further instructions. All ships had to fly a flag signal indicating their position in the convoy. If, for instance, your position in the formation was the third ship in the second column you would then fly a two-flag hoist of the numerals two and three. Each ship was given a specific time either to weigh anchor or to leave a berth and proceed to more open, wider and deeper water where the convoy would form up. Ships with numbers indicating that they would form the front line would be the first to leave. It could take hours for a big convoy to form up. If at anchor you could watch for the vessel timed before you to heave up and then follow on. The formation had to take into account the destination of various vessels, and those bound for Loch Ewe and the east coast would usually be on the portside. Oil tankers were the most vulnerable of all vessels and in an attempt to protect them they were usually placed in the middle of the convoy. This was not always effective for when the U-Boats began hunting in packs they would often infiltrate the convoy on bright moonlight nights with devastating results. Later it was decided to try and conceal which type of vessel they were and false wooden housing was built with a false funnel amidships to try and disguise them.

On one bright moonlight night when on a westward crossing in a smooth sea, the silhouettes of the surrounding vessels could be seen quite clearly. Before darkness fell there had been warnings of U-Boat packs being in the vicinity and gun crews were put on action stations.

At some time around 4 a.m. a loud bang was heard and there were fears that a submarine had infiltrated the convoy. After a night such as this it was usual when daylight came for the officer on watch to look around the convoy with binoculars to see if there were any empty spaces in the formation. This had to be done as soon as the visibility would allow for if there had been casualties the spaces would soon be filled by vessels closing up. Looking on this occasion I could see that we were all there but one vessel further down the line in the next starboard column had damage on her port bow. It transpired that an over-zealous gun crew on a ship well astern in our column thought they had spotted a U-Boat and had fired a round from their 4″ gun. Range and direction were a little out but no serious harm was done for the damage was high up on the bow and as we were sailing westwards to the USA all ships were in a light condition and were consequently well out of the water.

When on passage, signals from the Commodore vessel were sent by flag hoists if general or by Aldis lamp to individual vessels. The speed of the convoy indicated at the commencement of the voyage was kept flying until altered. If the speed was set at say 8 knots then a two-flag hoist would show the letter 'K' and below, the numeral '8'. A keen look-out had to be kept for any alteration in speed or course. Other signals sent out were 'close up', 'try and maintain station' and 'make less smoke'. This last was directed to coal burning steamships of which there were many. On a clear day this smoke could be seen for miles. It was hard to control for a lot depended on the coal you were burning and the firemen feeding the boilers. There was one signal regarding smoke which was directed to all ships instructing them to 'make smoke'. It meant that the smoke-making canisters kept near the stern were to be set off and thrown overboard to create a greyish smoke screen to help your bid to escape a surface attack. There was also the signal to 'scatter' which meant that you were to steer any course and take independent action to avoid the present danger of enemy attack. Both these signals were sent by the armed merchant cruiser *Jervis Bay* when she steamed out to meet the German battleship *Admiral Scheer*.

Just after mid-day all ships in the convoy were expected, weather permitting, to hoist flag signals indicating their noon position, as determined by morning longitude sights and noon latitude. It was of great interest when looking at other vessels' declared positions, to see where they reckoned they were or if we were the only one in step or vice versa. It was important that clues or signs were not left to indicate that a convoy had been in a certain area. Stoke-hold ashes normally dumped overboard at the end of each watch were kept until it was dark. Galley refuse and empty food cans were put in empty forty-gallon drums hung over the stern which could be up-ended to spill the contents by means of a small tackle. On some ships a canvas bag was used which had a trip rope around the bottom which, when pulled, would open up the bag and drop the contents. A submarine, seeing signs that a convoy had been in the vicinity, could pass messages to others who might be in a better position to mount an attack.

Radio silence was essential. The ship's radio station was manned for twenty-four hours but the only transmissions would be if attacked or in some other extreme emergency. Private radio sets belonging to crew members were not allowed to be used when at sea. Tuning the set could cause oscillations which could be picked up by the enemy and a bearing obtained. Every one with a set was put on their honour not to use it, but later it became necessary to collect all sets and keep them locked up until the end of the passage; any hidden sets were to be given, as the authorities worded it, the 'Hammer Test'.

Sailing in convoy was not easy and keeping station could at times be most difficult. The distance between columns and the distance to be kept between vessels in line was discussed and decided upon at the conference and this was stated on the information sheet. No two ships could sail for any length of time and remain the same distance from each other. It could depend on size, draught, weather and above all the engine revolutions required to maintain the speed as instructed by the Commodore. Frequent checks had to be made to determine if you were gaining on the vessel ahead or falling back. The height of the mainmast from the waterline of all vessels had been given but whereas naval vessels and some of the larger ships had range finders most of us had to rely on taking a sextant angle to find the distance off. After a few shots you had a good idea what the required distance looked like and with careful observation could keep in station. Some vessels had a critical speed which the engine could not be run at and they would be constantly moving up and down the line.

There were no revolution counters on the bridge and the only means of increasing or decreasing the engine speed other than by using the engine mechanical telegraphs which showed Dead Slow, Slow, Half and Full Ahead, and the same astern when the handle was reversed, was to speak directly to the engineer on watch. On most pre-war ships this was done by blowing down a voice pipe which had a whistle at the other end near the controls. After contact was made the engineer would be asked to increase the revs by a certain number or decrease them as was required. No conversation was needed. The only reason you were blowing down the pipe was to say 'up two' or 'up four' or down as necessary. There were times that when increasing revs to close up on the vessel ahead you found that you were gaining too quickly, perhaps because she had at the same time reduced her revs. We had no brakes so other than ring the telegraphs you would ask for a large reduction, pull out of line and find yourself sailing alongside your next ahead. There was always this up and down movement. Strict formation could never be kept. It was just the same if you were in the front line. The Commodore had decided at what speed we should proceed but it didn't follow, supposing the speed required was 8 knots, that the revolutions needed to achieve this speed were the same on all of the vessels. The front line could at times be very ragged. If an aerial film of a large convoy could be speeded up you would see the amount of movement going on between ships.

If stationed in the middle of the convoy there was this feeling of having company, like neighbours with ships all around you. But if in an outside column then on one side there would be complete emptiness and extra lookouts were the order of the day. The last ship in line also had to keep a good lookout stern for if the convoy were slow the modern submarine would be able to overtake and shadow it until night time and then attack.

This thought gave an added incentive to keep up but inevitably there were occasional stragglers, mostly with engine problems, who would be easy game for any marauding U-Boat or enemy raider.

Keeping station at night could be very trying. A lot depended on the weather and cloud formation. On a clear moonlight night the silhouettes of the other vessels could be seen, but this also was an ideal situation for U-Boats hunting in packs to infiltrate the convoy. It was surprising how you could, after a while, distinguish 'blacker than black' from just 'black'. At first, when ships were sailing blacked out with no mast-head or port and starboard lights, they were allowed to show a stern light which regulations decreed should be only half the power of the other lights, and shown over an arc of 135°. As the war progressed even this limited illumination was deemed to be too much and the stern light became a blue light shaded and shining directly downwards onto the water. When watches were relieved there were many things to hand over other than the course and speed and weather conditions. The oncoming officer would want to know if we were gaining or falling back on the vessel ahead. If you could see the blue stern light then you were in contact. Some vessels at certain speeds and draught had what was called a whining and singing propeller. It was very audible, like a whale calling to its young, and you would certainly know if you were getting too close.

After being weeks at sea, staring into the blackness could have a temporary effect on the sight of the watch keeping officer, especially the 2nd Mate who always kept the midnight to 4 a.m. watch which was always in darkness. I had an experience of this when I was serving in that role. One morning, about 2 o'clock,

I suddenly realised that I wasn't seeing anything, no blacker than black shapes, no blue stern light, nothing at all. I blew down the voice pipe to the Captain's bedroom and he came on the bridge immediately. After explaining my symptoms I was sent below to rest. Before the watch was over I had recovered and was able to hand over in the normal manner. This only happened once but I wonder how many other officers had a similar experience.

Trying to keep station in the winter months in severe gales and in a ballast condition was surely the hardest task of all and became, at times, impossible. Many convoys became scattered because of the Atlantic storms. With the vessel pitching and rolling violently in the mountainous seas the stern would lift out of the water and leave the propeller to thrash madly around. In these circumstances no progress was made at all. These conditions could prevail for days and it was quite a strange feeling to realise one morning when daylight came that you were all alone. When the storms abated the escorts, if there were a sufficient number of them, would attempt to round up the missing flock and bring them back into the fold. It was not always possible to reform into one convoy and sections would band together and proceed.

In these severe conditions there was some consolation that the enemy would be having a bad time too, keeping him well below the wave height and therefore restricting his capability. The course being steered before darkness fell was the one to be maintained, but in the long winter nights the wind could shift, the seas build up and in normal times, the course would be altered to ease the strain on the vessel. The flashing of Aldis lamp signals to and from vessels in a large convoy in the middle of

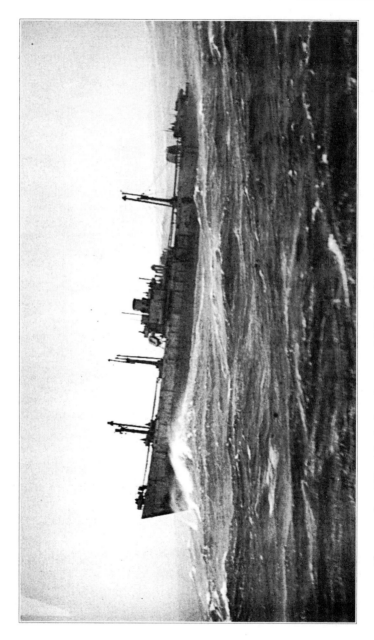

Above and p. 189, Admiralty pictures of Liberty ships in heavy seas on Russian convoys. (Imperial War Museum).

the night would have been tantamount to declaring our position by radio.

Fog presented a real danger. Fortunately it did not persist during the whole of an Atlantic crossing. It was prevalent in certain months around the British Isles and off the coast of Newfoundland, an area where most convoys made their way. Sound signals were permitted but the best innovation was the introduction of the Fog Buoy. This was a wooden contraption in the form of a cross. It had a metal scoop fixed to the bottom end of what you could call the long section. A bridle attached to each end of the crosspiece was shackled to a length of line paid out from the stern. When towed through the water the scoop sent a spout up into the air to a height of about five feet which could be clearly seen. You would be looking for the fog buoy if you suspected you were gaining on the vessel ahead. An ideal situation was if you could keep the buoy in sight at a safe distance on the bow, but it meant keeping a constant eye on the buoy and many alterations of speed.

Alterations of course were many during a passage, some for weather but mostly to avoid the convoy being intercepted at a later stage if the course could be monitored. Signals had to be made indicating the new course and the time of the alterations. There was a little confusion at times if frequent alterations were made and the signals not correctly read.

To ensure that all ships acted together, a plan was devised whereby ships would have pre-arranged sets of zig-zag courses with times of alterations, listed as No. 1 plan or No. 2, 3 or 4 etc. The only signal needed then was to declare the plan to be used. They were all different, showing various degrees of course, alterations and duration of each leg. Changes could be at 20 minutes or 45 minutes. The only mistake that could be made was if the officer on watch was busy with some other duty and missed the time. To ensure that this situation did not arise a zig-zag clock was introduced. This was an ordinary looking wheelhouse clock with the outer rim fitted with contacts which could be moved to any position on the dial. When the hands of the clock touched the contacts a buzzer alarm was set off which could be heard anywhere on the bridge. The contacts would be placed in accordance with the zig-zag plan to be put in operation and all ships would, hopefully, act in unison.

If ever the occasion arose when the Captains had to give orders to abandon ship and take to the boats they had instructions to destroy or dispose of all documents relating to the vessel and the convoy system. A canvas bag was provided which was heavily weighted at the bottom and had numerous brass eyelet holes punched into the canvas to allow maximum entry of water when thrown overboard. It would sink immediately. The Masters and Senior Officers were also advised not to wear their uniforms of rank when in a lifeboat. Some were callously shot before the U-Boat left the scene. It takes quite a few years of sea time gaining experience and shore leave studying to reach senior rank in the Merchant Navy. If these officers were fortunate enough to be picked up and returned to the UK they would most certainly return to the sea and man other vessels being built. Getting back to Britain meant that after a short survivor's leave you would be joining another vessel and heading straight back into the affray. Many merchant seamen survived as many as six or more sinkings and still went back to sea. The submarine could not take on board prisoners, so you might say that all is fair in love and war. As early as 1940 Admiral Dönitz, the

German Supreme Commander, had ordered his U-Boat crews to rescue no-one and have no care for survivors.

In the early days of war it was known that some U-Boat commanders had behaved in a humane way after sinking a merchant ship. There were stories of advice given as to the best course to steer to make the nearest landfall, and I heard of one lifeboat being towed for a certain distance and pointed in the right direction. Later on when the British Navy had gained the ascendancy in the Battle of the Atlantic and the U-Boats were on the ropes, as you may say, things became very ugly.

Medical facilities on British merchant ships, other than those carrying passengers, consisted of a medicine locker, a book entitled *The Ship Captain's Medical Guide* and the possession of a First Aid Certificate by each navigating officer. The certificate was issued by the St. John's Ambulance Brigade. We could not have dealt with any serious injuries suffered by crew members as the result of a prolonged and savage attack by the enemy. Despite the introduction as the war went on of more advanced drugs and pain-killers we could hardly have coped.

In peace time a passenger ship would, if in the vicinity, go to the help of one of its less fortunate brethren when called by radio, and advice could be had by calling a shore radio station if in range. Radio silence made this impossible so it was very comforting to know that when in convoy the naval escorts would have doctors or medics on board according to their size.

Later on came the introduction of 'rescue ships'. These were small merchant vessels fitted out specially to rescue survivors and treat injured and sick seamen. They were not involved in the carriage of cargo so could be switched from one convoy to another as deemed necessary. Their station was at the rear of the convoy and they were vessels of sufficient speed to be able to rejoin after completing their mercy mission.

When bound for the Mediterranean from the USA in American convoys vessels had to merge into two columns before entering the Straits of Gibraltar. As vessels began to close in and drop back to get into line the American escorts would be steaming at full speed across the rear, closing ships in and almost pushing them into the gap ahead. It reminded me of sheep dog trials with the destroyers racing from side to side until all the ships were in and the western end of the Straits was closed.

Chapter 9

Defensively Equipped Merchant Ships (DEMS)

D EFENSIVELY Equipped Merchant Ships. That is what we were called when provided with some kind of defensive weapon. At first it was the 4″ gun mounted at the stern after a suitable strengthening of the deck and structure in that area. The fitting of the gun was started as soon as war was declared and took place in many ports. It was said that these guns had been kept in storage since the end of the last war, but that was not too long before. Machine guns were mounted on the wings of the navigating bridge, and vessels with beautiful teakwood polished wheelhouses had them encased with concrete slabs as protection against low-flying enemy aircraft. The machine guns fitted then were Hotchkiss, Lewis or Marlin. I seem to remember that the Marlin had twin barrels.

At first the 4″ gun was manned by the ship's crew with a naval gunner in charge and a deck officer in attendance. As more armaments were introduced more naval personnel were required. Some medium-sized cargo ships had as many as twenty naval gunners on board. This was particularly so during the African, Sicily and Italian Campaigns, and then there would be a petty officer on board. The naval gunners were from the Royal Navy Reserve but not all guns were manned by them. There were also sea-going soldiers who belonged to the Royal Maritime Regiment and they usually manned machine guns and larger anti-aircraft weapons. This did not exclude some of the ship's personnel from being involved. Many, like myself, had taken gunnery courses, and held certificates of passing. My first experience of soldiers on board was when we were moving from one section of docks to another across a river. A lone plane approached and four gunners, who had been put on board carrying their own machine guns, ran on deck and opened up. They didn't hit the plane but managed to shoot away the ship's main radio aerial. This was before the formation of the RMR and they would be completely out of place on a ship with its many obstacles of derricks, guys and purchases.

On the *Fort Maurepas* we had a 4″ low angle high angle gun aft with two 12-pounder anti-aircraft guns, one aft and one on the fo'c'slehead. There were also eight smaller anti-aircraft gun emplacements in other strategic positions. The most heavily armed or, should I say, the most defensively equipped merchant ship I sailed on was the *Edward Bruce*. She was fitted with a 4″ LAHA, two 12-pounders and eight highly efficient Oerlikon AA guns in specially constructed emplacements, two on the fore deck, two on the after deck and one on each corner of the amidship accommodation block. There was also a rocket firing device which was placed on the after gun platform. It was a dome-shaped rocket launcher with two racks holding six rockets, one on each side. It was operated from inside and was presumed to be bulletproof. The operator sat at controls which could turn the dome in any direction, alter the angle of the racks and launch the rockets by means of two foot pedals, one for each side.

Accommodation became a problem when the gun crews were increased. The average pre-war cargo ship or tanker had no spare accommodation so extra housing had to be built. In cargo ships it was usually by using some of the cargo space in the shelter deck which was just below the main deck. A proper entrance and stairway was built and port holes placed in the hull in line with the new quarters. Ships built during the war had provision made for carrying extra crew. The two Liberty ships I sailed on had ample accommodation, for they not only had gunners on board but also signalmen when under the American flag and in ordinary circumstances would carry more crew than a British merchant ship. British manned Liberty ships carried no more crew than that prescribed by the Department of Trade in peace time and certainly no signalmen, whose job had to be done by the officer of the watch.

A number of submarines were sunk by merchant ship armaments and enemy planes shot down into the sea. Even if unsuccessful or not even used, having them on board created the feeling that at least you could hit back.

Many ships were sunk by enemy mines, which were laid in strategic waters and approaches to ports. At first they were conventional floating mines which were dealt with or swept by the Royal Navy mine sweepers who were called upon to clear the same area many times. Then came the devastating magnetic mine which at first there was no answer to. Without making contact the mine would be drawn towards the ship by the vessel's own permanent magnetism and this would cause the mine to explode, in most cases with fatal results. To combat this a system was introduced called 'degaussing' which involved passing an electric current around the ship which would neutralise or reverse the polarity in the permanent magnetism in the ship's steel structure, and dispel any attraction from the mine. The cables were fitted in channels welded to the ship's frames so as to completely encircle the vessel. Power was controlled in the engine room and switched on only when required. The fitting meant spending a few days in dock and on completion a yellow cross was painted on each side of the ship just below the bridge. I was never sure what this was for. Did it mean that if approaching a known magnetic mine area the ships with the cross would go first and those not yet 'done' would follow? The symbol was soon forgotten and painted over as all ships were eventually degaussed.

There were other means thought of to combat the enemy and reduce the danger of torpedo attack. Some were good and some, in my view, not so good.

The *Edward Bruce* was fitted with anti-torpedo nets. This was a device aimed at protecting the main part of the hull from being hit by a torpedo. It was only fitted on cargo vessels with engine and accommodation amidships. It would not be possible to fit the nets on tankers because of their particular deck lay-out with flying bridges and walkways above the main deck and the absence of winches. The principle was to have a steel net hanging in the water some distance from the ship's side. Four very tall booms were lowered horizontally from each side of the fore and aft mast housing. A heavy chainmail steel net was winched along a travelling wire from the after boom to the forward one and hung vertically in the water by means of weights. The nets stretched for more than half of the ship's length and if hit by a torpedo the explosion would not penetrate the hull, and it could possibly be deflected. The *Edward Bruce*, being a Liberty ship, had all the accommodation in one block amidships so it could be a protection against personal injury. When in use however there was a lack of speed and manoeuvrability. When not in use the booms were stowed in a vertical position fore and aft with the nets, wires and weights lashed at various heights to the after boom. With this extra top weight the vessel was most uncomfortable when in rough weather and in a ballast condition. On one occasion in very bad weather during the night the lashings on the port side became loose and with the ship rolling heavily eventually came adrift and the net and weights were swinging about wildly. It was quite an operation to re-lash the gear. This was done by myself and the Bosun. We climbed up the outside of the net and passed a wire by stepping round each other until it encircled the net. It was then led down to a winch on deck and drawn tight. It was quite a job in the dark and at one time we must have been hanging over the side of the ship. During the whole of my time on the *Edward Bruce* I only twice was required to lower the booms and rig the torpedo net gear and this was a practice drill when in convoy.

Someone had the idea that you could ensnare enemy low-flying aircraft by throwing a length of wire up into the air into which the plane would fly. Each end of the wire was attached to a parachute and when fired they would go in different directions with the wire stretched between them and then slowly descend. The drill was to press the buttons or switch the lever five seconds before the enemy plane passed overhead. How anyone could determine the speed of the aircraft approaching I don't know. If there were more than one and coming from different directions, what then?

Another contraption was the Holman projector. It was a type of mortar and operated by steam and so was only fitted on merchant ships with steam power. I had first-hand experience of this strange weapon when in the *Lancaster Castle*. It had been welded to the deck close to the hatch coaming of our after hatch which was No. 5. The chamber was angled outwards and was operated by a foot pedal. Steam was taken from the line running aft to supply power for the cargo winches and the steering gear which was situated right aft below the poop deck. To operate the projector a live grenade was dropped into the chamber and when the pedal was pressed the steam entered and forced the grenade out and high into the sky; or so it was supposed. On an outward bound voyage across the Atlantic it was decided that we would try our new acquisition out and see how effective it was. So as not to waste our supply of grenades on just a practice we found that an American beer can was exactly the right size to fit the chamber. We had some left over from our previous run. At that time our cans were not opened by a pull ring but were shaped like a metal polish can with a screw top. The beer was disposed of in the normal way and the empty can filled with an amount of sand to make it equivalent to the weight of the grenade, and the cap was then replaced. With one man at the pedal and another ready to drop the can in I gave the order to 'Fire'. Just minutes before this, and unknown to the gun crew, a flag hoist from the Commodore had gone up ordering an emergency alteration of course of some sixty degrees. The steering gear started to work overtime as the wheel was suddenly put hard over, and it needed all the steam it could get. What steam was left went to the projector and as the pedal was pressed our make-shift grenade came out of the steel tube, rose about five feet and dropped on the deck alongside us. I never had cause to use it again and it was more or less forgotten. It was hard enough to hit attacking enemy planes with conventional anti-aircraft guns which could be angled and rotated in all directions.

The great war-time comedian Tommy Handley had just as good an idea. He proposed covering the whole of the Western Approaches with green paint. Then when the U-Boats came up to charge their batteries their periscopes would be covered with paint. They would not know when they had surfaced and would carry on rising and thus would be shot down by Coastal Command aircraft!

Barrage balloons were used in an attempt to keep enemy planes at a height at which they could not drop their deadly cargoes accurately. They were placed in strategic positions around cities and important buildings and factories. East coast convoys were unique in that each vessel carried its own barrage balloon. It was quite a sight to see ships, usually in columns of two, sailing close inshore heading north or south with their balloons high above them. Southbound convoys started at the assembly anchorage off Methil in the Firth of Forth. I remember one early morning when waiting for daylight in order to weigh anchor and proceed as planned, loud noises and voices were heard as an MFV inshore fishing vessel manned by naval personnel came alongside and attached our barrage balloon to the handrail on the after deck. It wasn't too heavy and was walked by a number of hands and connected to the wire on the after-mast cargo winch and then raised or lowered as required. It was taken off at Southend before we headed up river to our discharging berth. At sea it was raised and lowered as instructed by the Commodore. It no doubt served its purpose in obstructing low-flying aircraft.

There were many changes of colour in the painting of merchant ships during the war. First it was grey, just ordinary grey as used by the Royal Navy, known by us as the 'grey funnel line'. For a little while some ships had a brownish superstructure and grey hull. Then we were coated in a lighter grey and afterwards a darker shade. Finally all structures above a certain height, which included masts and funnel, had to be painted white. I suppose it was assumed that a white mast sticking up above the horizon on a clear day would not be seen, but a grey one would. I couldn't see the logic in this and didn't understand the reason for the changes but it must have made the paint manufacturing companies happy, and others involved.

When the white paint was introduced I was serving as Chief Officer on the Liberty ship *Edward Bruce*. This meant that most parts of the net defence booms and heavy lifting derricks which were stowed vertically and a good proportion of the funnel now had to be painted white. The Silver Line who were managing the *Edward Bruce* had in peace time a distinctive livery with white masts and derricks, and a white funnel with blue top and a blue band lower down. As the *Edward Bruce* had a strengthening steel band of about six inches wide welded around the funnel four feet from the top, I decided to paint it blue. This could have been taken as showing the colours of those who were paying our wages, or it could be just pride in our ship, but it proved its usefulness when returning on board in a harbour full of this type of vessel: you just looked for the one with the blue band to find your own Liberty.

SS Edward Bruce taken from a model made by the author. This shows white paint at a certain height on masts, funnel and torpedo-net defence booms.

Whoever supplied the white gloss paint to the *Edward Bruce* must have been of a generous nature, or maybe there was some arm twisting, for our allocation was greater than the quantity required to comply with this new instruction. However, it did not go to waste.

Although the accommodation on these vessels was very good the alleyways and stairways were a little drab with everything being painted in the standard grey. This was not what we had been used to in British merchant vessels so the extra paint was put to good use and operation 'Brighten things up' began.

On a voyage to New York all the officers: deck, engine and radio, joined in during their off-watch periods and soon things looked very different. The transformation was amazing with everywhere looking brighter and somehow larger.

When the New York pilot boarded as we reached the harbour he had to enter through the accommodation and climb up three steel stairways to reach the wheelhouse. He remarked how clean and bright the interior looked and how different it was from that on other Liberty ships. Despite the repetition, it was again 'pride of ship'.

Some of my memories of those dark years are not connected with any particular ship but are more of a general observation.

I am from a seafaring family with father and grandfather having been to sea and was one of four brothers who had made the sea their career. During the war there were also cousins and one uncle serving in the Merchant Navy. Considering that from 3 September 1939 4,786 merchant and fishing vessels were sunk with the loss of 30,000 Merchant Navy lives I think my brothers and I were very lucky to have survived. We all had our various experiences during invasions, surviving enemy U-Boat and battleship attacks and being torpedoed and yet we all came back. In contrast to this it must have been heartbreaking for many married couples with one son who was called up and in no time at all they were childless. I remember after one short leave I was saying goodbye to my mother. She said, 'I expect to lose one or even two of you, I don't know which, but God bless you and keep you safe.' She said that she prayed for us many times no matter where she was and even in the small room. We did have one loss: the uncle serving as a 2nd Engineer Officer was declared missing lost at sea after his ship was torpedoed in the Atlantic.

As the war progressed and more and more ships were being sunk, lifeboat equipment, survival rations etc. were constantly being up-graded to ensure that seamen who had seen their ship and temporary home disappear beneath the waves would have a chance of surviving in an open boat until hopefully they were picked up.

There were some remarkable stories of endurance. Two young men, I believe from a vessel called the *Anglo Saxon*, were in a boat for weeks. She was sunk by a raider south of the Azores and west of Cape Verde Islands. They were eventually rescued and landed in the USA. Fate dealt a cruel blow on one of them for after rehabilitation he went to Canada to join a British vessel sailing from Halifax, Nova Scotia to the UK. During the passage the ship was attacked and sunk and he did not survive. The longest recorded survival was that of a Chinese crewman who was reputed to have lived alone on a raft for 120 days. He was picked up somewhere near the Bahamas and nursed back to health in the United States. At that time Chinese immigration into the USA was prohibited. It had been so before the war and I remember that when I was in American ports with a Chinese crew we had to have three guards on board day and night to ensure none of them went ashore. After making a complete recovery this brave survivor was rewarded by being granted American citizenship. A happy ending and a much better one than that of the previous story. There were many Merchant Navy personnel who returned to sea after being torpedoed three or more times and I believe six has been recorded, and young boys of sixteen were still joining the service. The rations in the boats of concentrated foodstuffs, vitamin tablets, condensed milk and medical supplies, together with distress rockets, were vital for any hope a crew might have if left in mid ocean. So it is with sadness that I record this shameful incident which happened when leaving a British port to sail across the North Atlantic.

Normal practice when leaving port was to swing the lifeboats out when clear of the docks and locks. They were bowsed in to stop movement as the ship rolled or pitched and the releasing gear and lowering tackle were made ready for instant use. Covers were taken off the boats and the contents checked. On this lamentable voyage the officer assigned to this duty reported that the boats had been rifled and all food rations, medical supplies, etc. had been taken. We could not possibly proceed like this and after reporting the matter were ordered back into port to replenish the missing items. It also meant missing that particular convoy and having to wait until the next grouping of vessels and escorts. Black markets have always flourished but I don't remember anyone being killed in consequence. Yet if we had not checked and had had the misfortune to be torpedoed in mid ocean many deaths might have occurred. This was a lesson well learned but one that you could hardly believe was necessary. Yet from then on whenever we were in port lifeboat supplies, everything except mast, sails, oars etc., was taken out and stowed in the wheelhouse which was kept securely locked.

The only form of identification merchant seamen had was a small metal badge with the letters 'MN' surrounded by a rope coil and the insignia of the top of an officer's cap badge above.

* * *

The war at sea started on the day war was declared with the sinking of the passenger liner *Athenia*. By the end of 1939, 96 ships had been sunk and by the end of 1940 a further 548. I remember once in the early days in a period known as the 'phoney war' I was almost elbowed out of a bus queue by some young army recruits because I was not in uniform. I wasn't so old myself, at twenty-four, but I had been at sea since 1931 and had made a few war-time crossings of the Atlantic at the time. Still, they were not to know.